# LANGUAGE IMPAIRMENT IN THE PRIMARY CLASSROOM

## A Practical Handbook for Mainstream Teachers

**Elizabeth Hoad**

# LANGUAGE IMPAIRMENT IN THE PRIMARY CLASSROOM

## A Practical Handbook for Mainstream Teachers

### Elizabeth Hoad

A division of MA Education Ltd

Teach Books Division, MA Education Ltd, St Jude's Church, Dulwich Road, London SE24 0PB

British Library Cataloguing-in-Publication Data
A catalogue record is available for this book

© MA Education Limited 2007
ISBN-10: 1 85642 349 2 ✓ ISBN-13: 978 1 85642 349 6

Printed by Athenaeum Press Ltd, Dukesway, Team Valley, Gateshead, NE11 0PZ

# CONTENTS

In this book, the use of he, him or his is gender-neutral and is intended to
include both genders. Similarly, for 'parents' please read 'parents and carers'.

# INTRODUCTION

Language and speech impairments are difficulties found in many children to a greater or lesser degree, but where there is a more severe difficulty primary teachers can often find themselves faced with a range of problems to deal with. These difficulties can be a challenge within a mainstream classroom context, and this book aims to give you some advice and strategies with which you can tackle the problems. Training for primary teachers in this particular area of special needs has not always been widely available; it is an aspect of special needs that has not always received the attention it deserves. Often it is not until a child with a Statement of Special Educational Needs (SSEN) in the area of language arrives in a school that many people are fully aware of the implications it has on the child, the class and indeed the school as a whole. This book may also make you aware of other children who have areas of need which may not merit such a high level of support, but whose areas of need should be addressed.

Language impairment has traditionally been seen as the preserve of speech and language therapists (SLTs), but increasingly mainstream teaching staff are required to support children with more severe needs alongside other professionals. As more children are included within mainstream settings, so the demands are being placed on teaching staff who may have little or no knowledge of the complexity of the needs of some of these children. The fear of letting these children down, of not being able to provide for their needs or knowing how to adapt your teaching so that they benefit within the classroom can be a hindrance, and this book should give you some simple strategies to put in place immediately. Parents need to have confidence in your ability to provide for their child, and for many it has been a struggle to have these needs recognised before they even reach school age.

This book is not just for newly qualified teachers, but for more experienced teachers who have a broad range of experience of children with special educational needs. The aim is to provide ideas and teaching opportunities to enhance what you already know and to enable you to build on this. It is designed as a handbook of practical ideas to improve the teaching of language-impaired children in order that their learning can be improved. Many of the suggestions and ideas should also help many other children in the class, and ultimately the hope is that your classroom will become more language-aware and rich as your confidence increases.

One of the common misconceptions about language-impaired children is that their learning is always going to be delayed or impaired as a result of their speech or language difficulty. For many children this is the case, but it is also true that for others, with careful teaching, their academic experience can be as valuable and productive as that of any other child. It is important to remember that these children also have other needs resulting from their primary need, most notably with their social skills. The effect that this can have on their experience of school is almost more important than anything you may try to teach them. There is a chapter devoted to tackling some of these issues and how you can address them with the whole class. You may find that this is the starting point of any work you do with these children, as their ability to communicate with other people, both children and adults, is key to their happiness and confidence. Enabling them to fit in with their peer group and develop a sense of self confidence is vital, and once they feel better about themselves you will begin to notice changes in their learning as well.

Within these chapters you will find a number of practical strategies and help which can easily be put in place in any classroom by any teacher, however experienced or otherwise. Look at the children you have in your class, prioritise their needs and put the relevant ideas into practice as and when they are needed. While some children will not need some of the strategies at any stage in their development, others will need them to be introduced gradually over time. Use the book as a handbook to dip into and to give you ideas as to how to direct your teaching more appropriately as the child progresses.

CHAPTER ONE

# AN INTRODUCTION TO LANGUAGE IMPAIRMENT

Having a child with a language or speech impairment in your classroom can be a daunting and worrying prospect if you have had little or no contact or experience with such difficulties before. However, there are many things that can be done to make the classroom and teaching more rewarding for you and the child. My aim is to provide practical help and tips which can be used with the whole class, and not exclusively for the language-impaired child. You will find that by adapting these ideas to suit your teaching and by accommodating the children's needs, you will have an exciting and inspiring classroom environment.

Many of these children can easily be turned off learning if they sense your worries and lack of confidence. They have more than enough to contend with already, unless they are brimming with natural self-confidence, and your attitude can make a real difference. It is true that many children with language impairment may have other learning difficulties, but this is not always the case. With a little understanding of their specific problems and a few ideas to develop their learning environment, you will find their language skills much simpler to manage within the classroom situation.

## LANGUAGE IMPAIRMENT OR DISORDERED LANGUAGE?

In this chapter I shall look at the difference between a receptive and an articulatory disorder and the problems commonly associated with each. I shall also define and explain the specific problems that you may come across. The terms 'specific language impairment' and 'language disorder' are commonly used to describe children with difficulties in acquiring and using language correctly. Generally speaking, a child with language impairment has a difficulty or problem which could improve as the child gets older. A language disorder is significant in its impact on a child's learning. It is a serious abnormality in the development of speech and language systems, and affected children have difficulties which need to be treated by an SLT or teacher right into adulthood.

Children with disorders suffer from significant stumbling blocks in the acquisition of language, whether it be speaking or understanding the spoken word. As a teacher you need to be careful about distinguishing the level of severity of the difficulty, as children can become experts at hiding their lack of understanding and will develop coping strategies of their own. This book should help you to identify potential problems for children with language impairments and disorders and will enable you to put simple measures in place to alleviate many of the difficulties the children face.

## DELAYED OR DISORDERED LANGUAGE?

Another distinction which needs to be made is whether the child's language is delayed or disordered. You will find that many language difficulties you are dealing with in a normal classroom situation are delayed language, which means that ultimately the child should be able to catch up with his peers with the correct support and encouragement. Disordered language is far more severe and needs far more support and advice to deal with within a classroom setting.

## RECEPTIVE AND ARTICULATORY DIFFICULTIES

A receptive language difficulty is one where the child has difficulties understanding language that is spoken to them. They have trouble understanding vocabulary, sarcasm, jokes, abstract concepts and the subtleties and nuances of language. One of the things I used to forget when I first worked with language-impaired children was that they easily misinterpreted common sayings and phrases which we use without even thinking, for example, "it's raining cats and dogs", or "you must be as quiet as mice", followed by a chorus of squeaking. An articulatory or expressive disorder is essentially one where the child has trouble forming speech patterns and sounds or has a stammer.

## SOCIAL AND EMOTIONAL DIFFICULTIES

Some children need a lot of social and emotional support as a result of their language or speech impairment, and this is almost more important to deal with as a teacher than any other difficulty. Children can be very unkind to those with something 'different' from the norm, and a child with a severe articulatory disorder can become very isolated and lonely. This seems particularly unfair when they may have no other associated problems. Language impairment is an issue which affects the whole class and, in a wider context, the school. For example, problems that need to be addressed arise in the playground, and all staff need to be aware of ways in which these children can be helped. A small issue can become far more severe if other staff members do not have a reasonable understanding of the communication difficulties these children have.

# CAUSES OF SPEECH AND LANGUAGE DISORDERS

There is a debate as to the causes of speech and language disorders, a medical approach and a linguistic approach. It is true that many children have had some form of medical intervention in their early lives. Bishop and Rosenbloom (1987) considered seven medically-based categories which could be the cause of a child's language impairment. These are structural or sensorimotor defects of the speech apparatus, hearing loss, brain damage or dysfunction acquired prenatally, brain damage or dysfunction acquired in childhood, emotional or behavioural disorders, environmental deprivation and also unclear aetiological disorders. It has been said that many of these categories are interconnected and have a bearing on one another.

There are many researchers who have categorised different types of language disorder linguistically, and these definitions are sometimes seen in the children's records or medical history. SLTs, educational psychologists or doctors do not necessarily use these labels in a child's case notes. The most common labels used are 'specific language impairment' or 'receptive and expressive language disorder' and the label is then qualified by how the child's language is affected as a result.

It is worth understanding some of the definitions of language disorder in case you come across them. I find Rapin and Allen, who name four types of disorder, suggest a useful categorisation.

- verbal auditory agnosia (word deafness, also known as severe receptive aphasia)
- phonological-syntactic deficit syndrome
- lexical-syntactic deficit syndrome
- semantic-pragmatic disorder.

It is also important to bear in mind that children may display characteristics which do not necessarily fit these exactly, and there may be other contributory factors which must be considered.

## Verbal auditory agnosia

Verbal auditory agnosia or word deafness is a severe problem where the child's understanding of language is very limited. It is a condition where a child has no apparent understanding of the spoken word, but may access language using some form of visual input. This has huge implications for the developing child, both educationally and socially. You often find that in the child's early years queries have been made about their hearing ability. Children with this form of disorder usually have to rely very heavily on the use of signs and symbols in order to understand and be understood. The most common signing used with these children is Makaton. Makaton signing is a unique programme which teaches communication, language and literacy skills to children with language and learning difficulties through a structured system. Many of the children I worked with used Makaton signing when they were very young as a means of communicating, but a child with verbal auditory agnosia would continue to rely heavily on sign language throughout their childhood and possibly beyond. Children with this form of impairment have usually been signing since they were very small and would usually be educated within a more specialist setting. It is possible to find classes where you can be taught Makaton signing, but the child's previous school or nursery should be able to pass on advice as to what they do. Another vital source of information and support is provided by the parents, and they are crucial in helping you to settle and teach a child with language problems. If you do not have a close working relationship with them it can make life more difficult for everyone. If there are problems at school or at home, they need to be communicated between you as they can impact one on the other.

This type of disorder is fairly common in children with Landau-Kleffner Syndrome, although they often have other language difficulties such as paraphasias, word-finding problems and difficulties with written language. You may find children display some of the difficulties associated with verbal auditory agnosia alongside another problem. It is hard to imagine the loneliness a child may suffer from with this kind of impairment and how frustrating it must be for them to be unable to communicate or understand others' meanings.

## Phonological-syntactic deficit syndrome

Phonological-syntactic deficit syndrome is far more common than verbal auditory agnosia. Generally speaking, a child with this has expressive language skills which are more impaired than their comprehension skills. Their expressive skills are more likely to be delayed rather than disordered. There are some experts who believe that often their comprehension skills are overlooked and that in fact they do have difficulties in this area as well. Adams (1990) argued this case and found in a study that

> *"children who appeared to have purely expressive syntactic problems in spontaneous conversation were found also to have receptive problems, when their syntactic comprehension was assessed with a structured task."* (Donaldson, 1995, p.29).

You will find that they only speak in short utterances that contain morphological errors. Another difficulty they face is with phonological contrasts which can make their speech unintelligible. They may have particular difficulty with the use of pronouns, prepositions, tense markings, plurals and other grammatical markers. This then has an impact on their written language and they may have trouble with grammatical rules.

## Lexical-syntactic deficit syndrome

Children with lexical-syntactic deficit syndrome have been very late to start talking but have no problems with phonology. They have severe word-finding difficulties with immature syntax. A child with this problem will display his difficulties most during conversation and may have trouble understanding what is being said, and in turn find it difficult to formulate a response without using fillers such as 'um' and 'er' or using inappropriate vocabulary. Some children choose not to have to speak as they will fumble and struggle to find the right words, and in a busy classroom it can be very difficult for them. However it is possibly one of the easier problems to deal with within a classroom as you can work on developing the child's self-esteem with the whole class. This in turn will help them to develop confidence when speaking. If they are not made to feel rushed, annoying or funny by staff and children alike, they can make good progress. They need to be taught vocabulary specific to the work they are tackling at the time, and giving them a printed list helps them as a prompt when speaking. Some children can develop their own self-help strategies over time, but others may just simply withdraw from a conversational situation.

## Semantic-pragmatic disorder

This is probably one of the language disorders most commonly cited on a child's notes, although there is currently much debate about whether this disorder actually exists. Semantic-pragmatic disorder is usually found in children who are on the autistic spectrum. They appear not to have any phonological, syntactical or morphological difficulties with language. Their use of language is highly inappropriate, although their comprehension and fluency are usually within the normal range. They can chatter incessantly, speak at cross-purposes or at a tangent to another, use echolalia, and will usually maintain a conversation for far too long or on an inappropriate topic. These children are unaware of their audience and of the reaction they would evoke, which can make for some awkward situations. Their verbal comprehension is often literal, so you need to be very careful about what you say to them. It can have serious implications both within the classroom and in the playground, where they may have real difficulties.

## PHONOLOGICAL PROGRAMMING DEFICIT AND VERBAL DYSPRAXIA

There are two forms of speech impairment which also need to be considered, and these are phonological programming deficit and verbal dyspraxia. With phonological programming deficit, the length of children's utterances is longer and unintelligibility of speech is a moderate to severe problem. Their speech-sound information processing is poorer than their potential to produce speech sounds. Coupled with this, their speech-sound contrasts are considerably reduced.

Verbal dyspraxia is also known as oral dyspraxia, articulatory dyspraxia or apraxia of speech. It occurs where

- the child's language is disfluent, laboured and severely unintelligible
- comprehension is usually adequate
- some children may even be mute
- expressive language is limited to short utterances or a few sounds
- there is difficulty saying single speech sounds, imitating strings of different sounds, and sequencing sounds to form words
- phonology is defective
- a child omits or substitutes sounds
- a child uses incorrect grammatical endings for words
- a child has trouble with fine or gross motor control skills
- a child has difficulty with sucking, licking, blowing and feeding.

As with verbal auditory agnosia, these children may need an alternative communication system such as signing. As they get older some children are able to achieve intelligible speech and mature language skills with the right support. Understandably, a child with verbal dyspraxia can be very frustrated and this may manifest itself in their behaviour.

## INTERVENTION

One of the problems associated with language difficulties is that they are often not apparent or dealt with for a long time. The earlier a child receives intervention and support from trained professionals, the more successful their integration into mainstream education. Many children slip through the net and you may feel that you have children within your classroom who have specific characteristics of language impairment without a diagnosis or specialist support. Not all children with language impairment will be on the special needs register or will ever find it a hindrance to their learning, but there are extremes where children are unable to access the curriculum. Some of these children will be in specialist provision, whether it be a school for specific learning difficulties or a language-resourced provision attached to a mainstream school such as the one I taught in. In the latter, the children will vary greatly in their abilities and their type of difficulty. All of these children are likely to be integrated to a degree within the mainstream school. It depends very much upon an individual's needs and sometimes it will change on a daily basis.

# ASPERGER'S SYNDROME

Autistic spectrum disorders have been mentioned briefly, and at this point it is worth mentioning a form of autism which you may well come across. Asperger's syndrome is a form of autism, and many children with Asperger's syndrome have disordered language skills. There are several factors which are characteristic of children with Asperger's syndrome and, although the list may seem rather overwhelming, it is a disorder which can be dealt with successfully within a mainstream setting, provided everyone is aware of the limitations and expectations for the child. These children are sometimes aware that they are different from other people, but they try to be sociable and do not dislike human contact. Generally speaking, they are interested in the world around them and will usually take part in lessons quite happily. Some of the hardest things for these children to understand are non-verbal signals, such as hand gestures, body language, or facial expressions. This has implications within both the classroom and the playground, and problems frequently occur because they do not understand this form of communication. It is astounding how much we rely on non-verbal signals as adults. It would be worth sitting and observing your classroom, or indeed the staff room, to see how much communication goes on without words being used. Like children with semantic pragmatic disorder, the children are unaware of, or not interested in, the reaction of their audience, although in general they speak fluently. This can lead to them rattling on and on without much purpose or interest in what is going on around them. Sometimes if you try to intervene or divert their attention elsewhere you may have little or no success. More often than not, once they are in full flow, they may change topic briefly and then revert to whatever they were talking about beforehand. On top of this, inappropriate remarks may be made and the child is oblivious to any offence that may be taken. Their speech may be over-precise or literal and when you speak to them they may take your words too literally. You have to be careful not to use idioms or sayings, as these are a real source of confusion. For example, if you say it's raining cats and dogs, they genuinely expect to see cats and dogs falling from the sky. This also means that jokes and metaphors are lost on them and can isolate them from the other children. Part of the social life of school is based on telling jokes and making each other laugh, and they miss out on this aspect of relationships.

A child with Asperger's syndrome needs routine and structure. A chaotic, disorganised and ever-changing classroom is unsettling and worrying for a child with Asperger's syndrome, and problems occur as a result. The same can be said for their home life, and any kind of change can be very unsettling. The beginning of each new school year, staff changes, or house moves for example, will all have a great effect on their happiness and behaviour and will impact on everyone around them. Some young children can impose their own routines and will stick rigidly to them. Simple tasks and routines within the classroom such as changing for PE, organising their books for a lesson and so on can be quite demanding. If they find a way of doing these things with which they are comfortable but may not fit your classroom routine, you need to consider whether you impose your expectations on them or work with them, perhaps negotiating a compromise between you. Giving these children a daily or weekly timetable to follow helps to lessen their anxiety and upset, but if something changes for some reason (and as teachers we know that not everything remains the same each week, for example, assemblies move, halls may be needed by other people) this can have serious implications on how well the child will cope. It is as if they need to know what is happening in advance in order to mentally prepare for it.

Some children with Asperger's syndrome can remember facts and figures really well but fail to use this information in an imaginative way. I worked with a little boy who was obsessed with dinosaurs and knew everything there was to know about them, but if I had asked him to try to record this information in an exciting way he would have really struggled. It is as if they can process and retain something that interests them, but taking this a stage further and using the information is impossible. Their hobbies and interests can become obsessive and will transfer from home to school, so it is important to help them to find a way of drawing a line between the two and distinguishing between what school is all about and how home is different. Imagining something in the future is a very difficult skill, and literature is hard to understand as it requires the imagination. Using hard facts and non-fiction materials is a good way to work with them first of all.

The physical manifestation of Asperger's syndrome is less difficult to deal with in school. There can be some clumsiness and parents may have noticed that the child has had difficulty learning to ride a bicycle for example. The child can sometimes adopt odd postures and use repetitive movements. One of the difficulties we faced with a child with Asperger's syndrome was getting him to change for PE and then enabling him to remove his plimsolls in the hall without getting upset. He would then only take part in one corner of the hall, but with encouragement and time and not pressurising him, he was eventually able to join in like all the other children. Demanding or expecting them to do something that worries or frightens them can have a negative effect and undo any hard work you have already put in. However frustrated or impatient you may feel, you must give them time and space (within reason) as it can otherwise lead to even more long-term problems and a lack of confidence and trust in you.

## COMMON DIFFICULTIES WITH LANGUAGE-IMPAIRED CHILDREN

There are several common difficulties that you will encounter when working with a child with any kind of language impairment. The following problems are not all apparent in all cases, but you will usually find that they have a selection of difficulties, such as

- poor concentration
- poor listening skills
- weak phonological awareness
- poor auditory memory
- word-finding difficulties
- poor vocabulary
- poor semantic understanding
- weak syntax
- problems with comprehension and expression of language
- morphological problems
- weak social and pragmatic skills
- delayed literacy skills.

One of the difficulties you will face in your classroom is that children with language difficulties can have very poor concentration and listening skills as a result, and this can cause real problems. Another difficulty faced by children with language impairment is a poor auditory memory, which is interlinked with the concentration problems and listening skills. The difficulties faced by a child with attention deficit disorder (ADD) are similar.

Language-impaired children's phonological awareness can often be weak, and this has an impact on their literacy skills. At one point I did a trial where I taught a child on a one-to-one basis and developed his phonological awareness. There was some evidence that his literacy skills were improving, but more time and a bigger sample of children were needed in order to determine the validity of this premise.

Word-finding difficulties have already been mentioned within the context of specific impairments. You may find that children suffer from this to differing degrees; it could affect them when speaking and not when they are completing written tasks, or only when trying to use vocabulary in a written context. There are several simple measures which can be put in place to help with word-finding problems, and these will be outlined in a later chapter. Alongside this difficulty, children may have a very poor vocabulary anyway. This could be due to a variety of factors such as limited language experience in their early years, the home background, poor auditory memory, phonological problems and literacy problems in general.

On the more grammatical side of things, a child with language impairment could often have poor semantic understanding, weak syntax and problems with comprehension and expression of language. Poor semantic understanding means that vocabulary is a problem area, especially when learning abstract concepts such as time. Children with language impairment often find difficulty with grammar, especially, for example, with word endings, word order and tenses. Word-finding and verbal reasoning cause problems too. These children can also have morphological problems, which means that their word structure or use of morphemes could be jumbled.

One of the most common problems is that these children may have weak pragmatic skills, and this can vary in severity. Social skills are a vital aspect of school life, and a child who struggles with this is already at a disadvantage. It is such an important area to deal with for the language-impaired child that a later chapter is devoted to methods and strategies which will help. There are a number of reasons suggested as to why these children suffer from poor social skills. These could be a lack of confidence, lack of experience or just poor awareness of other people. Pragmatic disorders also mean that children struggle with ambiguity and implied meanings, and their world knowledge is limited.

Arguably the biggest difficulty you may face as a teacher of a language-impaired child is their delayed literacy skill. It is true that their intelligence may not be affected by their disorder, but the fact that there are crucial missing links in their language development will ultimately have an effect on their ability to read and write. This may not be a major problem and could be overcome by early intervention, but a significant number of language-impaired children will continue to have literacy difficulties into their teenage years and beyond. It is therefore vital to give them as much support as possible to boost their self-esteem and ability to read and write. One of the biggest factors in a child's improvement is the feeling of self-worth and the belief that they can succeed. Once a language problem is detected, then work must be done to put the missing building blocks of language in place. The earlier this is done the better, although sadly many children reach infant and junior level before alarm bells ring. It is vital to ensure these children have one-to-one literacy support to give them every chance of making the most of their innate abilities. One of the luxuries of working within a resourced language provision is the level of adult support, but with tight budgets and staffing levels in a mainstream school, time may be limited. However, in the long term the benefit to the child and his education is invaluable. Small group support within the classroom can be organised to enable you to dedicate more time to these children. With careful planning and classroom organisation you can fulfil some of their needs without extra classroom support. However, there is no real substitute for one-to-one adult support and this is something you need to consider with the Special Needs Co-ordinator (SENCO) in your school. Involving the child's parents in your teaching objectives as much as possible is also important. This may be in the form of work they can follow up or practise at home, or even just by making them aware of what you are doing in the classroom.

The most important thing to remember when you are working with a child with language impairment is that however frustrated *you* may feel, the child is probably feeling ten times worse. My most memorable and rewarding times in a classroom have been with language-impaired children, and my life as a teacher has been richer and more enjoyable as a result of learning alongside them. It may seem a daunting task when faced with the unknown, but it can prove to be quite exciting when you find the key to unlocking children's potential. By using the suggestions contained in the following chapters, you may find your classroom is language-rich for everyone and that this may have an impact on the whole class.

CHAPTER TWO

# DEVELOPING CLASSROOM STRATEGIES TO IMPROVE LANGUAGE

A language-rich classroom is not just vital for children with language impairment; it is also very important for children without language difficulties. In such a busy world full of technology and fast-paced action, children need time and space to explore language and be exposed to words in as many varied and exciting ways as possible. There are many ways in which you as a teacher can make your classroom a more interesting and stimulating environment. In this chapter you will find strategies to enhance your teaching and the role your learning support assistant (LSA) can play within the classroom.

## TEACHER INITIATIVES

### Time to Speak

One of the most important things for children with language difficulties, whether they have an articulation difficulty or a more complex impairment, is to allow them time to speak. One of the things I found most difficult when I started working with language-impaired children was knowing when to correct errors and when not to intervene. It is very tempting to leap straight in when child is talking and correct what he is saying, or to interrupt a stammerer who cannot say the appropriate word. This is a skill which takes time and patience to master, but it is best to try to take your cue from the children. It is important not to embarrass them by correcting them in front of everyone else, even if you feel it is beneficial to their language development.

It takes a long time to feel confident in finding the best way forward for an individual. Talking to parents and previous teachers and finding out their strategies is important as it means there is some continuity for the child. The way in which you listen to children reading and knowing how and when to intervene is a good marker for your general dealings with them. Sometimes you could put words into their mouths that they do not want or you could misinterpret their needs if you step in too quickly. It comes back again to time and patience, learning alongside the child and ensuring that the child feels confident with you. You will find that you eventually become tuned to his language and will instinctively know how and when to intervene. Your behaviour will in turn influence the attitude and understanding of the rest of the class. This is not to say that you should treat language-impaired children any differently from other children, it just means that you must be sensitive to their language needs and be aware of the limitations this may pose.

There is a process of education which you as a staff, and the children in the class and school as a whole, have to go through. If we can enable others to stop, listen and give children the chance to speak, then many of the battles they face as a result of their articulation problems can be overcome. It may indeed take longer for them to explain something or understand what is needed of them, but we must give them this time in order for them to make progress.

## Breaking down instructions

Breaking instructions and general dialogue up into chunks of information and feeding them to the child a piece at a time can really help their understanding. One of the things I found when working with language-impaired children is that they often need time on a one-to-one basis to talk to you. The pressure of knowing there are lots of children around them listening to their request or conversation can make the whole situation more difficult. Try to withdraw slightly to enable them to have some breathing space. Time is precious in the classroom and you could argue that this time should be distributed more evenly among the rest of the class, but if the child feels he has your support and confidence, huge steps can be made.

## Self-esteem

It is important for self-esteem to value each child for what he is, and it is vital for both you and the class to understand this. You must never forget that the intelligence of language-impaired children is unaffected. They can be very sensitive to you treating them differently or excluding them from activities because of their problem. For example, assemblies and more public events beyond the classroom walls can be a daunting experience for any child, but do not suppose that just because speech may be a difficulty the child does not want to play a part.

## Discussion

Discussion forms an important part of the curriculum these days, whether in groups or a whole class situation. It could be all too easy to disregard a child with language impairment because you need a session where ideas and opinions are put across at a rate where the majority of the class is engaged and will not lose interest. It is important for children with language impairment to feel that their contributions are as valuable as those of any other member of the class. This requires almost endless patience from you and from the other children, but you must give the child a chance to contribute. Listening to and volunteering opinions and ideas will enable language-impaired children to feel part of the class, rather than being on the periphery because their language skills form an impenetrable barrier to normal classroom life. Praising their suggestions and contributions will give them the confidence to speak up again. Similarly, you need to be aware of the reaction and body language of the rest of the class in case the child is aware of restlessness and disinterest among his peers.

## Non-verbal communication

It is important to remember that communication is not just verbal. Drama sessions, mime and non-verbal communication can be equally successful in improving a child's self-esteem and confidence, and many children find a channel for themselves in these areas. One little boy I worked with had a severe articulation disorder and after some persuasion he joined the school choir. It was discovered that he could sing beautifully without stammering and this gave him a huge confidence boost. Taking a role in drama can help the children to distance themselves from the reality of their language difficulty; they are playing a role and this can be utilised to develop their confidence and their acceptance by other children. We should never stop children doing such activities if they want to take part. Exclusion can have a dramatically negative effect upon a child. It would be interesting to talk to actors and see what they are really like, rather than relying on the public persona we are used to. I am sure that many are not as confident or articulate as they may appear on stage or screen, but acting gives them a release from themselves to a degree. You may also find that some children with a language disorder are already very confident and would resent being sidelined or told they could not do something because of their language skills.

## LSAS AND THE ROLE OF THE SENCO

Your LSA or classroom assistant can play a vital role in helping a child who has a language impairment. You are generally too busy as a teacher to spend all your time assisting one individual, but the use of your other staff can make a big difference. It is important that the child is confident with both of you and feels he can approach both of you, whatever the difficulty. You do not need to have someone sitting beside him all the time. That would not be constructive at all. But you can arrange things so that help is there when necessary. Working within a group of other children with adult support enables the child to work more independently but with some supervision.

# Planning and target setting

Other staff are important in feeding information back to you about the child's learning, and their observations should play a part in your planning. It is vital to involve them in your forward planning and target setting on an Individual Education Plan (IEP). It is more than likely that they will be carrying out the majority of the work that you set within this plan, so they need to be confident to do what you plan and to be clear as to your aims and objectives. You should ultimately be making the decisions, but I found that many of the staff I worked with came up with suggestions or adaptations of the work in order to tailor it more specifically to the child's needs. You may find that this has to be re-addressed frequently. If you find it difficult to have time to speak to the other adults in the class, use a book to write messages to each other. For example, the working hours of staff who worked with me meant that I was already teaching when they arrived, so I would leave a list of what I wanted them to do until the time when we could talk. The book can be used as a record of work carried out, or merely as a means of communication.

# Special needs co-ordinator

The role of the SENCO is vital too, as children with more severe language impairment will generally have an SSEN. The SENCO should be able to give you some additional support and advice and, if necessary, give you some assistance in deciding on the areas you are going to target. During the academic year it would be a good idea to liaise with the SENCO on a regular basis, as the implications of language impairment are not just felt within the classroom.

# Other Staff

Assembly times, the playground and extra-curricular clubs mean that all teachers will come into contact with language-impaired children, and it is only fair to the other staff to make them aware of the difficulties the children face and the strategies you employ to help them. You must also consider lunchtime supervisors and any other staff who work in direct contact with the children.

# INSET training

If possible the SENCO and you, as the class teacher, could offer training for the rest of the staff (teachers and LSAs). A general awareness of the needs and difficulties of language-impaired children is important for staff development. You may find that other children within the school are displaying signs of language difficulties, and sharing your knowledge with them may help. They may even have devised strategies to help in their own classrooms which could be used and adapted by other staff. Even if they do not have language-impaired children in their classroom, many of these ideas could be used to make the classroom a more language-rich environment for all pupils, whatever their ability.

# CLASSROOM STRATEGIES

There are many simple things you can do within your classroom which will work to improve children's language skills. If you use any or all of these suggestions they should help any child, whether they have a language problem or not. These ideas are designed to be adapted to suit your purposes and individual needs. The other thing to remember is that you will need to take your cue from the children and their specific needs, because not all the ideas will work for every child.

## Word lists

At the beginning of new maths and science topics give the children word lists. When the Numeracy Strategy came into effect, I used to type up the vocabulary and print it out so each child had their own copy. I would also enlarge the list and put it on the board. This gave the children a prompt when struggling for the correct word and meant that they did not have to worry about the vocabulary, as well as learning a new aspect of maths. At the beginning of a session I would run through the vocabulary with the children and talk about the words they knew, checking which ones meant the same as each other. This meant that they could talk more confidently when carrying out mathematical activities, without struggling to find a word. If necessary, they can point to the word they need to use if they are finding it difficult to articulate the word. Similarly, when working on a science topic you could give the children a basic list to which they can add words as the topic proceeds. This could ultimately be made into a glossary.

## Job lists and timetables

Many children, whether they have a language-impairment or not, find it very hard to keep track of the work they are supposed to achieve. It helps to write a job list for a group or an individual either on a daily or a weekly basis. The children can keep a record of what they have achieved, and what they still need to do, without having to constantly ask the teacher or other children. There are many different ways you can do this, either in the form of words or pictures. The children will become more responsible for their own progress and you can focus their attention on short-term targets.

Another thing you can do to assist them is to provide a laminated timetable for the week which they can use to help to organise themselves. Using symbols rather than words to represent subjects may help, and colour coding works in a similar way. For children with problems such as Asperger's syndrome it would be a good idea to send a copy of the timetable home so that they can be prepared for the day in advance.

## Labels in the classroom

Some schools are not keen on labelling drawers, but with language-impaired children it is important. If equipment is clearly labelled, then they will be able to play a more active role within the classroom, helping to get out and put away items. Labels using words and pictures are even better, as the clues are all there to assist their reading and recognition of objects. These could be linked with the timetable; for example if a child has real difficulty organising themselves for specific lessons, draw pictures on the timetable of the items they need. Alternatively provide them with trigger cards for each subject, illustrating the books and equipment they need to collect before they can start the task. These pictures need to be replicated on the items themselves, so the children can match the two together. As their organisational skills improve, you will not need to be so obvious, but it does give them a head start. We all know what it is like to have a whole class sitting down to start a task while one or two children drift around, unable to collect what they need. This tactic should make a difference and lower your blood pressure at the same time.

## Hierarchies of words

Vocabulary can be categorised to help children to learn the most important words, or a key word to trigger their memory. This approach has been developed by speech and language therapist Dr Wendy Rinaldi (Language Concepts to Access Learning) and can be applied to many areas of the curriculum. The idea is to create a hierarchy of words starting with the most commonly used and working through to the least, for example: foot → heel/ankle/sole/toe → nail. The materials that you work through as part of a child's programme enable you to assess areas of weakness within his vocabulary. Once you have established the basis on which you are working, you can then teach in a more directed manner. When you have worked this method through for a while, it is fairly straightforward to adapt it to most topics within the curriculum and is a good way of helping children to expand their vocabulary. It should help them to learn new words and retain them by word association. Further mention of this technique is made in *Chapters 6 and 7*.

# Reading Material

Every classroom should have an extensive stock of fiction and non-fiction texts so that children can pick up a book whenever there is a spare moment. It is essential that you have material relevant to your current topic on hand so that it can be picked up and looked at without needing to go to the library.

Non-fiction is an excellent way of engaging a child who finds reading difficult. Short pieces of information text with pictures and illustrations are less daunting than a page of close-typed text. Although children with language difficulties may have trouble reading some texts, they should still have access to them. Picture books are a good way of encouraging them to talk through a story, and there are even books which contain no words at all. Discuss the pictures with them and ask them about what they imagine the characters are feeling and what they may do next. To encourage their own story writing, copy some pictures from an unfamiliar text and ask them to supply the story in a written or verbal form. This means they are relying on picture clues and can put their own spin on a story. It would be interesting to take a book they are familiar with and do the same to compare the results. How much are they influenced by what they already know? You can then compare their version with the real one.

Sharing books with adults and children is an excellent way of developing their confidence. Enjoying books is not limited to fiction alone and we must not discourage a child who is reluctant to read fiction. A successful way of presenting stories to others is to use puppets to tell the story. The children can make sock or finger puppets and use them to dramatise the text. Many children who lack confidence in their language abilities may find this a means of release; it is a puppet that does the talking rather than themselves. The same can be said for drama sessions, when children are acting out roles and not presenting their own personae.

# Dictaphones

Dictaphones are an invaluable resource and can be used very effectively in a classroom. Talking their thoughts, stories or observations into one can reduce children's fear of committing themselves to paper. Holding all their ideas in their heads while they painstakingly write out their work can be a nearly impossible task, so recording it in advance can help them to remember important facts. Dictating ideas to an adult to produce notes, which can then be used as a prompt as the child writes, is also a good idea. They can also be used very effectively to help a child learn spellings or times tables facts.

# Writing frames

When writing, give the children a writing frame with specific headings. These headings give the child a clue as to what they need to record next, and in the correct chronological order. Such frames could be created for a variety of subjects, for story plans, persuasive writing and scientific experiments. The children can organise their writing more effectively using these frames, and consequently their thoughts become more coherent. The prospect of recording a scientific experiment in words can be very daunting for many children, but for language-impaired children it can be a nearly impossible task. Another way to record facts is to use flow charts and diagrams, and this can also relieve the pressure to retain and use vocabulary. Stories can be recorded in picture form with a few words rather than long sentences. Making storyboards, such as those used by filmmakers when planning animated films, is another way of helping the children to plan the stages of their task.

# Question cards

During the teaching part of a session when the children are all gathered around, children with language difficulties tend to get forgotten or lose interest. To counteract this and to ensure that they are fully involved, use question cards. Give out small cards to them with a question mark printed on them. That means that you will be asking them a question in the next few minutes, or that they have to answer a question without you asking. This keeps them listening and means that they are just as involved in the lesson as everybody else. It helps to keep their attention focussed not just on you but also on what the other children are saying. This technique could also be used successfully with children suffering from ADD. The difference was quite remarkable when I tried this out in my classroom. Children who had previously sat back and expected other children to answer and play an active role in discussions suddenly had to be directly involved. Their interest was engaged instantly, and more often than not the work they did as a result was more successful.

# Target setting

Involving the children in their learning and helping them to set targets for themselves alongside your aims and objectives is very important. After each half-termly review of the children's IEPs, a system of target cards was devised in my classroom. We all felt the children needed to be more involved in deciding the targets we were setting for them and being aware of them. Consequently I used to make two target cards for each child each half term, one for literacy and one for numeracy. The children had to collect their target card at the beginning of the relevant session and have it sitting on the table beside them.

This meant that they knew they were concentrating on one specific thing, for example, recalling number bonds to five without practical apparatus, or spelling words correctly with magic 'e' at the end. This meant that, instead of feeling they had to get everything right, if they managed to do this one thing they had achieved a huge amount. The sense of being able to do something, however small, can work wonders for a child who struggles day after day with the implications of language impairment. The cards were kept in pockets on the wall with each child's name on it, so they could find them easily and return them at the end of each session. It also meant that any other staff teaching in the classroom (particularly supply teachers) were able to find them and were aware of the targets we were trying to achieve. Communicating the needs of children with special needs to other staff is not always possible, and this is a quick and effective way of doing so. At the same time you are able to give individuals a sense of responsibility for their own development.

These are just a few suggestions to help you to develop language within your classroom. Once you have some of these basic organisational techniques in place then more specific curriculum support will be easier to initiate. The most important thing to remember is that by giving the children access to books and the spoken word, both from the people in the classroom and from tapes, it will be a language-rich environment. Enabling children to talk to each other as they carry out technology and scientific work is also crucial, as they will explore the task through words as well as actions. However, establishing a good relationship with the children is vital so that they feel confident to practise and improve their language skills. Later chapters will discuss specific curriculum areas in more depth and will give ideas for developing language within these subjects.

CHAPTER THREE

# SOCIAL SKILLS

Social skills are a very important part of our lives and we take certain behaviour for granted. In the classroom, as in the outside world, there are specific behaviours that we take for granted and expect not to have to teach. For a language-impaired child many of these skills need to learned and continually reinforced. These children may appear to be rude, insolent and incapable of observing basic courtesies. Many children with language difficulties find it hard to understand the correct way to address people and have trouble recognising the different uses of language. In order to attempt to redress the balance, you will need to make time to teach social skills. Half an hour once a week for a focussed session should make some difference, and you will need to reinforce what you have been doing whenever you have an odd few minutes, for example at the end of the day, waiting to go into assembly and so on.

Spend time with the whole class doing things such as giving them different situations, for example, speaking on the telephone, requesting something in a shop, or introducing themselves to someone. Something as simple as a basic greeting and acknowledgement of other people can be a complex skill for a child to learn and it will need to be taught and reinforced. One of the mistakes people can make with children with a language disability is that of making assumptions about what they can and cannot do. Never take anything for granted, particularly when it comes to everyday use of language. Children can appear to be rude and abrupt, when it may be a simple case of not knowing how to address someone, or learning to wait to speak.

There are many ways of tackling social skills sessions and it would be an idea to vary what you are doing to make each session fresh and exciting. The following are suggestions of how you could set up these lessons, and examples of what you may need to cover.

## WHOLE GROUP

The most obvious way of teaching social skills is as a whole class. You may already have circle time, especially at junior level, and this can be adapted to cover social skills. It is helpful to ensure that the children are all able to see you and each other. The ideal is to have the children sitting in a circle so they can make eye contact with everybody. If moving furniture is impossible, you could do this in the hall, music or drama room and, in the summer, outside. The idea of being able to make eye contact with everyone is that you can tackle sensitive topics and everyone has to take an active role; there is no hiding beneath a convenient table nor the opportunity to fiddle with the hair of the person in front.

Whole group sessions could involve specific teaching, but lend themselves beautifully to discussions and game playing. You can tackle issues that have come up, such as incidents in the playground or classroom, and discuss how they could have been avoided or diffused. Use role-play to portray the incident as it happened and then discuss what went wrong. How did the language inflame the situation? Was it a question of misinterpretation or misunderstanding? Once the children have discussed this, decide on the appropriate language to use or action to take. When they are in a situation that could become unpleasant, what sorts of tactics could they use to calm things down? Would it be an idea to have some form of peer group mediation?

Discussions about other issues which concern the children are very important. Sometimes it may be a good idea to ask one of the children to be the chairman of discussions like these and for you to take a back-seat role. In this way the children may feel more confident about talking about sensitive issues without your interference. It may enable less confident speakers to contribute, but it is important to set ground rules. In order to prevent children from being shouted down, the chairman needs to maintain order and must be aware that he controls the discussion to a degree. Perhaps giving the speaker an object to hold to indicate that they have the right to speak would be a good idea. It introduces the notion of turn-taking and enables everyone to have the chance to put his point across without interruption.

Another thing that you can do within the whole class situation is to play games as a whole class. This will foster a sense of cohesiveness within the class and hopefully remove tensions and problems (even for a short time). You can play games such as wink murder, the bunny game and 'I went to the shops and I bought…'.

## Wink murder

For Wink Murder you will need a set of cards one marked with a large **M** for the murderer, one with a **D** for the detective, and the rest blank. Every child needs to be given a card but they must not show it to anyone or give any indication about what is on their card (easier said than done!). The children are asked who the detective is and are then told to start. The murderer has to set about subtly winking at one child at a time. If they are winked at they must 'die', quietly if possible, and try not to give away who winked at them. The detective has to try to spot who is the murderer and catch them in the act. It is a great game for bringing a class together and they can become quite proficient at demolishing their classmates once they become accomplished. The important thing it is teaching is how to make and maintain eye contact and pick up on non-verbal signals.

## The bunny game

The bunny game is equally important in teaching children to watch for non-verbal signals and to make sure they make eye contact. They need to sit in a circle and one of them starts off as the bunny, holding their fingers above their head and wiggling them. The child to their left holds up their right hand above their head and wiggles their fingers. The child to the right of the bunny holds up their left hand and wiggles their fingers. The bunny then needs to make eye contact with another child around the circle. Once eye contact has been established they point their fingers at them, passing the bunny to them. The original bunny and children beside him drop their hands and the new bunny and neighbours take over. This game can become fast and furious and great fun, as well as teaching valuable skills. The best way to play this is in silence so that the children can concentrate on observing and reacting quickly. It is usually the bunny's neighbours who have the most difficulty either holding up their hand or getting their co-ordination right.

## 'I went to the market and I bought...'

The aim of this game is to concentrate on turn-taking, memory and group dynamics. An accomplished class can become very supportive and helpful to one another and find ways of helping children to remember the list of things. Start the class off chanting 'I went to the market one day and I bought....'. The first child says an object such as an apple. The next child then starts "I went to the market and I bought an apple and an orange" (for example). The game then continues around the class until the list becomes very long. Hopefully the continual repetition of the list and the association the children make by looking at each child as they remember what they said enables them to recall more objects. Some children become very good at giving non-verbal cues when someone becomes stuck, by miming for example. The sense of achievement they feel if they complete the circle successfully is fantastic and can really bring a class together as a whole.

## SMALL GROUPS

Small group social skills sessions are more intimate and arguably more successful, although you cannot cover issues with the whole class. Groups of up to ten can work very well for some of the suggestions given later in this chapter. One major difficulty is that you have to organise your class so that you are not in demand from the rest of the children. One potential solution is to double up with another class at story time, one teacher to read to the majority of children while you take a selected group from each class. Another alternative is to keep a group out of assembly one day so you can give them your undivided attention. There are many aspects of this kind of teaching and learning which need to be covered within a small group setting where it is quiet and uninterrupted.

With a small group you can organise the furniture so that the children are sitting in chairs in a circle. This may lessen their ability to fidget and fiddle. It is vital that you plan your social skills programme and slowly develop the skills you are teaching. To this end you must start each session with some form of standard warm-up activity and then ask the children to recall what you covered in the previous session. So, for example, if you are tackling conversation, your warm-up could be a formal greeting time from one child to another around the circle:

> *"Good morning, Thomas, how are you today?"*
> *"Very well thank you. Good morning, Eleanor, how are you?"*

and so on.

Once your preliminary warm-up is complete, you need to move on to the main teaching aspect of the lesson. Your main aim is to get the children actively involved as much as possible and not to talk at them; they will remember the lesson better if they are doing something. This part of the lesson could be practising something from previous sessions and developing it further through role-play, games or discussion. Role-play is a very valuable aspect of social skills sessions, as you can tailor the scenarios very specifically. It is not such a 'loose' form as drama, as the children are not being asked to be imaginative. They need to think about real-life situations, not something that is unfamiliar to them. When planning your programme, use your initiative and take your ideas from the problems you see your children encountering on a daily basis. Once your main teaching objective has been achieved, conclude the session with something the children are all involved in, such as a game. It is almost like a wind-down period and does not necessarily need to be directly linked to your teaching focus.

## Meeting people, greetings and introductions

Think back to the first time you met the children with specific language difficulties and try to remember your first verbal contact with them. Did they say hello, stare at you or say something inappropriate? Meeting someone new can be a daunting experience for many people at the best of times, so imagine how difficult it must be for a child who has no idea what the conventional and acceptable forms of greeting are. You will need to teach them about the difference between greeting adults and children and how those greetings vary as you get to know those people. You need to ask them about what they would say to their family as they leave or arrive at home. How different would that be compared to arriving at school and greeting the headteacher? Ask two children to enact the two situations, one as the adult and the other the child. What would they expect to hear if they initiated the greeting and vice versa? Practise this scene with all the children so that they all have a turn. Just watching and listening to others doing this is not enough. To ensure they have absorbed all this information you need to see them practising. As with everything in this chapter, you will need to return to work you have done earlier in the term until you are sure they have actively retained and used the information. If necessary, prime the other teachers and ask the child to go to another class to fetch something in order to practise their new-found skill.

Introductions are another tricky area, especially when the children are starting a new school year or changing schools. They need to be able to introduce themselves and not to be afraid to speak to other people. Teach them how to remember other people's names by repeating them, for example:

> *"Good morning, my name is Mrs. Hoad and I am your new teacher."*
> *"Good morning Mrs. Hoad, my name is Thomas."*
>
> *or*
>
> *"Good morning, may I take your name?"*
> *"Good morning, my name is Thomas."*
> *"I am your class teacher and I am called Mrs. Hoad."*
> *"Mrs. Hoad."*

There are many situations outside school when they will need to give their name, and you can practise these once they have established the basics. You can also go on to developing introductions even further by discussing how they would get to know another child. How would they impart information about themselves to another? What kind of information is appropriate to pass on at the introduction stage? All of these aspects are minor minefields which can cause huge problems for children and can ultimately determine whether they make friends or not.

## Telephone conversations

Telephone conversations can be a real problem, as children have no non-verbal cues to pick up and are fully reliant on what they say and what is being said. Sometimes it is important just to teach them how to listen attentively to what is said at the other end and respond appropriately. The best way to do this is to have two children sitting back-to-back so they cannot see each other and to conduct a conversation on a given topic or for a specific reason. They will need to learn how to reply to a ringing phone, and how to listen for the information that is given when they answer. This is particularly important when answering the telephone, as they will need to be immediately aware about who is calling them. Is it their friend or someone asking for another member of the household, and so on? Similarly when they are making a call they will need to check the identity of the person they called and give information about who they are and why they are phoning.

Once the preliminaries are over, you then need to move on to how to conduct a conversation on the telephone. They need to think about the kind of language they would use to speak to someone they know and how they would speak to a stranger.

The final stage is to teach them about taking messages and how to end a conversation appropriately. It is surprising how many children without language difficulties have trouble with taking messages and ending conversations politely. This aspect may take a long time to teach, but it is worthwhile. One school where I taught had two children manning the office telephones at lunchtime and they were required to take messages and fetch staff if they were needed. It is vital in this case that the children can give a good impression as no-one knew who would be phoning, it could have been a parent or an inspector.

# Shopping

Shopping is another tricky area for children with language difficulties, as you cannot always just pick something up, pay for it and leave. Even if the shopping experience were that simple, children would still need to use language to greet the assistant as they pay and as they leave. You will need to practise different scenarios with them, for example supermarkets, post offices, newsagents and butchers. Each different place will need a different kind of greeting, request or response. You will need to help them to greet the shopkeeper appropriately, request a specific item or a list once they are more confident, and then conclude the conversation. Once they become more used to dealing with a basic transaction, you can challenge them by getting the shopkeeper to ask for more detail. For example:

> *"Good morning."*
> *"Good morning, how may I help you?"*
> *"Please may I have 1kg of apples?"*
> *"Which would you prefer, Granny Smith or Braeburn apples?"*

The children buying should not necessarily know that a question would be asked of them, so they need to think on their feet and reply appropriately. This is far closer to a real-life situation and is the kind of thing that could cause them to panic, get flustered and be unable to continue the conversation successfully.

It would be an idea to ask the children to tell you all the different ways they can think of to greet someone in a shop and how they are likely to respond. Similarly, they can think of all the different questions they could potentially be asked in each situation. Once they have established this, then they can practise with more confidence, as they will be used to hearing the different words and phrases in a more familiar setting. It would be fantastic if you had an opportunity to take the children to a local shop to practise their new skills. It would give them a huge confidence boost and help you to know that they can carry these skills into real life. It is also important to tell their parents that this is what you are focussing on, so that they can continue the work at home and encourage the children when they are shopping together. Many people think that children with language impairment do not want to speak out, but the reverse is often the case. If they have the vocabulary and the opportunity, then they will want to practise, if encouraged and supported.

## Conversation (beginning, ending, listening)

Many children with language difficulties find it hard to start and maintain a conversation appropriately. This is an important skill, as they need to converse with their peers as well as adults. If they are able to talk appropriately with their peers, it can make all the difference to their ability to make and keep friends, an essential part of growing up and arguably one of the ways in which they may be able to overcome some of their difficulties. Small groups are best for this kind of session, although you could introduce the lesson as a class and then split into small groups of about four children to hold a conversation. You could concentrate on beginnings and endings to start with, and discuss ways of doing this. It may be a good idea to give the children examples of good and bad conversation beginnings and ask them which ones would be appropriate. For example, would they expect to start a conversation about the football match the night before by saying, 'the referee's decision was dreadful'? It would be far better to start with comments such as

*'Did you see the match last night?'*
*'What an exciting match it was last night!'* or
*'I am so tired as Mum let me stay up to watch the football last night.'*

Take time to rehearse this, as it is important to make a good first impression in a conversation. There is no point in being the most interesting or witty conversationalist if you cannot begin in an appropriate manner. Similarly, children must understand that if they interrupt or change the subject to conclude the conversation, or stop listening, no one will bother to talk to them again. Once the beginnings and endings are established firmly in their minds you need to concentrate on the content of the conversation. Many children with language impairments show signs of the 'cocktail party syndrome'. In a nutshell, this means that someone will talk endlessly about a topic of no real interest to anyone, does not demand any meaningful response and is seemingly oblivious to other people's boredom or disinterest. It is very difficult to help children to unlearn this kind of behaviour; all you can do is give them pointers about how to share a conversation with someone. Teach them how to allow someone an opportunity to ask questions, how to ask those questions themselves and how to change the topic of conversation without appearing to be rude. It is easiest to tackle this during a session as examples appear, rather than attempting to provide examples here. Your instincts will tell you when to intervene in a conversation and ask the children what they could or should say next. Ask them to suggest alternatives and then use what they have learned in the conversation.

If the children are really uncomfortable about this sort of scenario, start off by asking them to suggest topics which they feel confident about. Once they are happy about talking in a group then start giving them topics to discuss that may prove more challenging. If you have the opportunity, make time to sit down with your language-impaired child or children once a week on an individual basis and talk with them about anything they like. This kind of practice with someone they are comfortable with is vital. They know that you will not be rude to them or walk away if you get bored. If necessary, set a time limit using an egg-timer so that they do not feel too overwhelmed by the prospect.

## Language for different situations

This has been covered already to a degree with the sections on greetings and conversations. However, it is important to spend time asking children about differences in vocabulary and when it is appropriate to use certain language. You could make a list of slang terms or jargon that they use with their friends. Ask them whether or not they would use this kind of language in the classroom and if not, why not. Discuss the kind of language they would use with friends, family, teachers, strangers or the police. They need to start to appreciate that people use language in different ways and in different situations. To illustrate this, you could initiate a conversation about something familiar, such as football. Then ask the children to imagine they are talking about it to a different group of people. Get them to have a conversation taking on a different role as necessary and at the end ask them how each version differed and why. What was different about their language and why did they adapt it?

## Playing games

One of the most difficult skills to learn as a young child is how to share and take turns. For many children with language impairment this skill is still underdeveloped, as they have not had the means to communicate effectively in certain situations. Therefore it is very important to help them to develop these skills by playing games and helping them to learn how to win and lose. Their use of verbal language and body language can be critical to whether they have successful experiences with other children. It is important to supervise these situations closely and to intervene where necessary and help to teach them appropriate behaviour. Similarly, they need plenty of practice sharing tools and equipment. You could role-play situations in order to show them how certain language would be aggressive and annoy other children and how this could be tempered to create a different outcome. It will take time to improve the situation, but you will gradually notice a subtle difference if you make a concerted effort to change their language.

## What would you do if?

This would be an interesting exercise for the whole class to do as it will test their resourcefulness and can show surprising results. Give the children different scenarios such as, 'you have lost your Mum in a supermarket, what would you do?', 'you have lost your way and need directions,' and 'you find somebody's keys, what would you do?'. This should lead on to some very interesting discussions about whom to approach and why, what information would you have to give or ask for, how to think of other people's needs and how your actions can affect them. Role-play would be the best way to tackle this kind of activity after a discussion, as you can get the children to create the situation and see how they would put their language skills to use. You will need to ask the others if it was clear what the initial problem was, whether each party gathered the right kind of information and if they could solve the problem from this information.

## Asking for help

During your sessions on what would happen in certain situations, you may cover the possibility of children getting lost somewhere or asking someone for help. However, it is important to teach some of the following skills in separate sessions, as they are vital for their confidence when in an unfamiliar situation. They will need to be taught how to ask a stranger for help and this will include knowing who it would be safe to approach. In the case of some autistic spectrum disorders, children would ask the most inappropriate people for help, so it is important to teach an awareness of stranger danger at the same time. Once they have found a suitable adult to help them, they will need language to communicate the difficulty they are in. This will, of course, vary according to the situation, but again role-playing different situations will help. It may be necessary to spend time teaching children the obvious and practise saying their name, address and telephone number. It is surprising how many children are unable to give this kind of information accurately. Even if this were all they could communicate successfully, it would be a great help to them in a difficult situation and ultimately cause less anxiety and distress.

## Following directions

This will follow on from learning to ask for help, as the person they ask may well give them verbal directions or instructions to follow. Many times during the school day children are given instructions about what to do. They are expected to assimilate this information, retain it and then act on it. It is a good idea to give them a set of verbal instructions about doing something or going somewhere and seeing how they react to this information. Build up the list of instructions you give one at a time and help them to develop their confidence to follow them accurately.

## Playground scenarios

The playground can be an emotional and physical battleground for a child with language difficulties. Simple misunderstandings that could be defused ordinarily can become inflamed purely because the child is unable to articulate their apology or feelings. You will need to practise with the children about how to ask to join in with a game that is under way and how to initiate a game. It is also important to teach them how to use language in a non-aggressive way and to be able to apologise when they bump into someone.

Another problem can be that children take comments made to them in passing far too personally and they may react badly. They need some time to understand that reactions can be instantaneous and not necessarily meant personally, however it may seem. This process is difficult and you may need to monitor their playground activity very carefully. It is also important to speak to the other staff, both teaching and non-teaching, who are on duty so that they are aware of the child's difficulties. There are many instances of 'rudeness' or inappropriate responses to adults, which are not necessarily meant, and the staff need to understand their weaknesses and respond appropriately.

## Emotions

Understanding emotions and interpreting them correctly can be very problematical for children with language difficulties. You may need to do a lot of work on looking at facial expressions on pictures and in real life and asking the children what the people are feeling. Stick to very simple expressions to start with, such as happy, sad or angry, and then move on to more complex ones later on. You will need to talk through what makes people feel this way, what makes them happy or sad and ask them to show you the expression they would use if they felt in a certain way. Some children may only be able to relate to a picture, so provide them with simple line drawings on a card for them to use as a reference.

The next thing you will need to work on is teaching children how to give and accept compliments. This is more important than you realise in a classroom, as children comment on each other's work. Some children can find it very hard to take praise or a compliment from anyone, least of all a child they don't know well, or a teacher. They can retreat into themselves and close up or react badly. It may sound a little extreme, but it is worth taking time to consider. Try to get them to praise each other's efforts on a daily basis and ask them to comment favourably when they see work displayed around the school. They will need to listen to appropriate and inappropriate language and decide which is better.

On this note, it is also worth taking time to ensure they are able to be polite and use socially acceptable conventions. This will include being able to thank people correctly, both children and adults, and to use the right sort of language for this. They may also need to learn how to make an apology without offending or upsetting someone further. All the subtle nuances of this sort of language which we take for granted can be a minefield for children and you will need to take time over this.

## Classroom etiquette

The expectations of children within a classroom are quite high, and as teachers there are certain behaviours that we expect and take for granted. It can therefore be quite a challenge when faced with a child who has no concept of the rights and wrongs of their own behaviour. These sorts of social skills need to be taught gradually, and over time things should improve. Work on one thing at a time, such as respecting other children's space, sitting on the carpet at the beginning and end of the day or simply raising their hand when they need something. Many of the other issues mentioned above will have an impact on their behaviour in the classroom. You must remember that often any bad behaviour is caused because they are confused and struggling to understand the world around them. Teaching them social skills should help to alleviate some of their fears and anxieties.

This is by no means an exhaustive list, but should give you ideas as to how you can develop social skills within your classroom. You will find the needs of the children are very different from one class to another, so follow their lead. You may set out a structured programme of what you aim to cover, and find that other more pressing issues crop up during the term. Do not be afraid to divert from your initial aims, but if something needs to be tackled, deal with it as soon as possible. The other important thing to remember is that these sessions need to be recorded on the child's IEP. They are relevant to their specific need and should be recorded formally.

CHAPTER FOUR

# IMPROVING ATTENTION AND MEMORY

Attention and memory difficulties permeate through all levels of educational difficulty, and many of the suggestions in this chapter could be used to help any child with attention difficulties. There are varying degrees and levels of difficulty in this area, but the suggestions can be adapted according to the severity of the problems you encounter. Attention and memory are inextricably linked, because without attention nothing would be remembered. We have to pay attention to something in order to commit it to memory, whether it is stored within the working or long-term memory. There was a far greater emphasis placed through the National Numeracy (DfEE 1999) and Literacy Strategies (DFEE 1998) on chanting and repetition of facts as individuals and as groups, thus enabling information to be maintained within the working memory. There are many advantages to this, but it does not tackle the more long-term difficulties faced by children. It also does not take into account the fact that, no matter how many times something is chanted and apparently learned, a short time later it could be forgotten. Some of these strategies will give you the opportunity to help other children with attention difficulties.

A poor visual memory has implications for the way children learn. For example, babies learn about the world and their carers through visual stimuli and recognition of these stimuli. Vocabulary is learned through associating objects with the spoken word. If their visual memory is lacking, then word associations will be lost, causing a delay in language acquisition overall. At a later stage, as children are learning to read, we often use pictures to associate with letters of the alphabet and sound patterns. As teachers we rely on a child's visual memory to recognise these connections. As a result we need to modify our teaching to enhance children's abilities and play to their strengths. As with many aspects of learning, children will only learn if the building blocks to help them learn are in place. There is no point ploughing ahead if a child needs fundamental work on his visual memory skills. Time spent working on this aspect will pay dividends in the future. We must not forget that for some children, learning and remembering things is a skill which needs to be acquired and is not an innate ability.

Attention is the process that underlies all our activities, whether we are consciously or subconsciously attending to something. We know from working with children that attention improves with age, as indeed does memory, and we know that the cognitive processes of children with general learning difficulties do not usually develop at the rate of other children, and even come to a halt before they reach maturity. The attention problems of small children will therefore be apparent in these children right into adulthood. As a teacher there is nothing more frustrating than a child or children who are not attending and are consequently disrupting the class. Their difficulty has an impact on the whole class and needs to be addressed as soon as possible in order for everyone to benefit. Attention difficulties come in a variety of guises; a short attention span, a low boredom threshold, distractibility, ADD/ADHD, over-focused attention, and selective attention.

Children with general learning difficulties tend, on the whole, to be fairly distractible. This is particularly apparent when looking at autistic children and their classroom environment. Invariably, small workstations are seen around the class effectively screening off the child from normal classroom distractions. Maintaining concentration in a noisy classroom is extremely difficult for many children and, from my experience in the language unit, the children frequently felt disorientated and confused when surrounded by thirty-odd other children. As a result, a distractible child is unable to take in what is being taught and will consequently fall behind in all aspects of his work.

Children with short attention spans have under-focused attention, whereas children whose attention is very fixed and single-minded have over-focused attention. Autistic children tend to be at the extreme end of this spectrum, becoming totally obsessed with one thing.

This may all sound rather alarming, but there are many simple strategies that can be put into place within the classroom to assist children with attention and memory difficulties. Some are very practical and others relate to your own language and behaviour, which can be modified to help improve their chances of developing these skills.

## STRATEGIES FOR DEVELOPING LISTENING AND ATTENTION

### Visual cues

Using pictures, symbols and labels around the classroom will help to focus a child's attention. Most classrooms are covered with brightly coloured displays with labels or some form of interactive element. These can be used to good effect to direct a child when teaching them, giving them something to focus on. Therefore a display board can become a useful teaching tool. Labelling where equipment is kept will help children's organisational skills. Similarly, if you use a colour co-ordinated classroom timetable and match the colours, it could potentially make life simpler, for example art materials could have red labels on drawers and art on the timetable would be coloured red. Pictures and symbols can serve as a prompt when reminding children of work already undertaken or work to be completed at a later date. Before the start of each lesson you could give the children who have problems with paying attention a cue card indicating the things they need to collect, for example, maths book, pencil and ruler. This could take the form of words, pictures or both and would just serve as a focus for their attention. Once you have completed the teaching aspect of a lesson and the children disperse, then there is a temptation for children with attention difficulties to wander around and these cue cards can really help.

## Classroom position

The careful positioning within the classroom of a child with a limited attention span is vital to help them to concentrate on their work. Avoid sitting them near a window or door where they can see the outside world, as this is usually a recipe for disaster. Similarly, avoid placing the chair where you read stories, teach from or sit with groups with its back to a window. The children would look at you but would be very easily distracted by anything passing by; even the movement of birds or trees would be enough to pull their attention away from you. When choosing a position for sitting with the children in front of a flip chart or board, think about what else they can see from their position. Is it looking onto a busy art area or another classroom? For many autistic children, the only way to focus their attention is to give them a purpose-built workstation, which effectively screens them from general classroom activity. Moving tables can achieve the same effect so that the child is looking away from a window or towards a wall, with few children nearby. In this way it is possible to place a child away from distraction which can be caused by unnecessary sights and sounds.

## Repeating name

Repeating the name of a child within a classroom situation can refocus their attention. The frequency with which this is necessary is dependent on the severity of their learning difficulty; some children need to be reminded only occasionally whereas others need constant support. A child's name is an instant trigger to his attention as it is used from birth and is recognised immediately by the subconscious. During literacy sessions many children tend to drift off unless they are regularly involved in the lesson. A strategy which has been employed very successfully in maintaining the concentration of children has been to ask an individual three questions in succession. This has the effect of ensuring that the child has to have been paying attention throughout in order to answer correctly. The rest of the class also all sit up and pay greater attention just in case they are the next 'victim'.

## Short, simple, clear explanations

Giving short, simple and clear explanations is important for all children within a classroom whether they have a poor attention span or not. We can lose children by giving lengthy detailed instructions; tasks are muddled, completed incorrectly or misinterpreted. Consequently the rest of the lesson will be spent going over and over what has already been said. This is very frustrating for you, takes your time away from teaching or assisting and makes the classroom feel chaotic and disorganised. If necessary, write out the key points or steps of a task on a board or on cards and put these out on tables in order to jog their memory.

## Real objects

We are all encouraged to teach children through seeing and doing, so using pictures or artefacts as much as possible will help children to remember the subject matter you are teaching. Visual stimuli make lessons come alive and become interesting, for example teaching history by talking can be deathly dull, but bring in a few artefacts or pictures and instantly the children are engaged and interested. They can begin to visualise things for themselves. In the same way, teach art by physically demonstrating a technique. Some children learn numeracy skills more effectively if they have practical apparatus to use. If children find it hard to take in words and retain them in the correct order, then showing them something helps them to commit stages of a task to their memory.

## Praise and encouragement

This is almost the most important factor in maintaining a child's attention and self-esteem. Motivation is the key to a good working relationship with children whatever their needs or difficulties. A child who constantly receives negative attention and is never praised has nothing to strive for, whereas the child who is praised and encouraged has a far greater chance of achieving. By encouragement and positive attention on your part, the child will develop a good working relationship with you and will be more interested in what you have to say and will find it easier to concentrate within the classroom.

## Key words

Children with attention difficulties need to be able to focus on something visual or verbal in order to attract their attention. The importance of using names has already been mentioned, and using key words as distracters is helpful. For the individuals in your class who have the most severe difficulties, agree a set of words between you that they listen for. For example, 'look', 'listen', 'go'. This goes back to the importance of short simple sentences. A single word has more effect sometimes than a whole string. Once you have gained their attention, then use longer phrases or sentences to explain, request or discuss something with them.

## Listening goals

As well as having key words which the children are listening out for, agree listening goals with them. During teaching sessions the key word approach is not so appropriate, so before you start teaching tell the children they are listening for a specific phrase or words, for example in a literacy session on poetry, 'I want you to listen for words rhyming with shoe'. When the children have heard this, they must respond in an appropriate manner and join in with the discussion. It will help them to focus on what is being said by you and the other children, and hopefully more of what is being taught will be absorbed as a result.

## Consistency

It is important that children have some form of structure and consistency in their working lives. This is even more important for children with attention difficulties and, if possible, the strategies you are using should be shared with anyone else who may work with them, for example helping parents or supply teachers. Many difficulties you have with children displaying these areas of weakness are made worse, however temporarily, by other adults who are unaware of how you are already working together. Children's confidence and trust can be easily broken if your hard work is not maintained. Leave a bullet point list of your 'tactics' for each child in an obvious place, so that other staff can easily see what you are doing. The child will have more confidence in you and other people they may work with.

## Break tasks into smaller parts

The importance of using short, simple instructions has already been emphasised. The same applies to tasks you expect children to achieve. Break each task into smaller parts and praise the child every time one part is achieved. Choose some kind of recording system between you so they know what has been achieved and what remains to be done. If you do a simple flow chart or print out for longer tasks, the child can highlight or tick them off as they complete each stage, for example:

1. Collect maths book, pencil, ruler, tape measure, box of objects
2. Write the date and title *'Measuring Objects'*
3. Write the name of each object in a list
4. Measure one object at a time
5. Record measurements beside the name.

This is clearly a very simple example, but as the children get older this tactic can be developed and extended according to their ability. Older children could have a book in which you write a daily job list so they know exactly what you expect them to achieve. Using this method will only work with a lot of support to start with, and the child must know that you will follow up each day and check what they have been doing. If children are aware that your attention is not on them when you have set them parameters to work within, then they will fail to perform. Children with attention difficulties do not need 100% of your attention, but they do need to know that there is some comeback if they do not do what they have been challenged to do. Some form of reward such as stickers is essential to bolster their ego and confidence once they have achieved your target.

## STRATEGIES FOR DEVELOPING MEMORY

### Overlearning and rehearsing

Most of us find that in order to commit something to memory, some form of repetition is required. How many times have you seen someone in the supermarket deep in thought or looking heavenwards trying to remember his list? In the classroom we can see children using all kinds of strategies to help them remember things, for example, muttering under their breath. We need to teach children overlearning strategies, and this is being reflected in mathematics with the repetition of number facts. A multi-sensory approach is vital as we do not all remember things in the same way. Saying things aloud, writing them down and so on all help us to remember things and can help them stick in our memory. Learning spellings using the Look, Cover, Write, Check method is very effective. Some children find that talking spellings or number facts into a Dictaphone can be a very effective way of helping them to remember. Replaying the tapes at regular intervals is essential to maintain the memory. It is essential with all children to revisit previous work in order to test whether they remember something. Some children retain facts in their short-term working memory and may consequently do very well in a spelling test, but when tested at a later date cannot remember the words. You need to teach them overlearning skills and it is essential to rehearse what they have learned regularly, in order to give them a chance to retain information in their long-term memory.

### Visual prompts not verbal instructions

A child with memory difficulties can have great trouble remembering basic routines. In this instance it would really help to use visual prompt cards to remind them of what they need. The use of a colour coded daily timetable using colours to denote classroom time, PE and so on has already been mentioned. As well as helping children to attend to something, it should help their memory in the long term. Picture prompts around the classroom can also help children to visualise and remember where things are kept. When learning to read and write, nursery and infant teaching often focuses on learning the letter names and sounds of the alphabet by using pictures or actions that trigger the child's memory, for example, Jolly Phonics. Another way of doing this is by associating the letters with names.

## Visual mnemonics

For some children using mnemonics can help them to remember facts. Most of us learned the rhyme '30 days hath September', and sets of words using the initial letters to help, for example, 'Richard of York Gave Battle In Vain'. In the same way some children can remember spellings like this. You need to start being creative and find other keys to their memory. One favourite with children when learning the vowels is, An Elephant In Orange Underpants. They can draw a picture to remind them and this provides an excellent cue to the memory at a later date. I heard an LSA teaching a child how to spell 'because': 'big elephants can always understand small elephants'. Many staff members have their own personal favourites and it may be worth asking everyone for their ideas and pooling them as a staff. It is important not to forget the expertise and strengths of other staff members, and their advice is on hand and free.

## Reminiscence

Children can be trained to improve their memories by practising remembering, but it is a process which takes time and constant practice. You can reminisce in a number of ways. For example, in social skills sessions you could ask the children to tell you what they did at the weekend. The rest have to listen until everyone has spoken and then individuals have to remember what the others have done. They all need to listen and retain what has been said. In this way they are being trained not only to listen well, but also to store information in their working memory. It may take some time before this is truly successful, but it is worth the effort. Once they start learning to listen in this way and use the information they have heard, then this skill will ultimately spill over into other aspects of their school life.

By retrieving information regularly, children are learning to reminisce. Playing games such as 'I went to the market...' and Kim's Game helps them to remember. 'I went to the market' involves one child saying "I went to the market and I bought an apple", for example. The next child in the row or circle then says "I went to the market and I bought an apple and a banana," and so on. It becomes increasingly difficult to remember the shopping list, but by repeating the list and saying it aloud constantly it should start to stick in their memory. Many children find that they remember the item of shopping better by looking at the child and associating them with what they have said.

Kim's Game involves placing a set of items on a table in front of the children and asking them to look carefully at them. Once they have looked hard, cover the items up with a cloth and while the children have their eyes closed remove an object. Ask them to open their eyes and then uncover the objects. The children then have to say what is missing. You can vary this by removing more than one object or adding a new object to the set. There are many other games available in toyshops which work along the same theme and can help children with their memory skills. Not only are they developing their memory, but also they are also practising turn-taking, concentration and are improving their social interaction with others.

## Participation in skills and routines

Maintaining a routine and a structure to the day is important for most children, especially when they are very young. For children with attention and memory difficulties it is especially important to do this. Try to keep certain aspects of the day the same, particularly in the morning. Take, for example, registration routines. Children can easily become disorientated and confused and they need to start the day positively. Similarly, at the end of the school day everyone is tired and possibly frustrated, and it is important to try to maintain some semblance of order among potential chaos. If the day ends badly, that is what the child will remember before arriving at school the next day and it can have a negative effect on both behaviour and confidence.

## Verbalisation

The importance of multi-sensory learning has already been mentioned, and verbalising what the children are learning is crucial to retaining something within their memory. There is a far greater emphasis within the curriculum on chanting and saying things aloud as a class than there used to be. Writing spellings down at the same time as saying them out loud means that most of the senses are active and will assist in the ultimate retention of the word. Repeating times tables and number facts on a regular basis will help as well. Encouraging the parents to be involved in this as well will also make a difference to the child. The knowledge that both home and school are working on the same things and in the same way, ensures consistency and a more successful result in the long term. Overlearning and rehearsing this information is vital afterwards.

# Immediate recall and repetition of information or instructions

As an adult, I know that I have listened to something or read something and it has gone straight out of my mind. After attending courses or lectures it has helped me to tell someone what I have learned shortly afterwards, while it is still fresh in my memory. It may be helpful to get a child to record multiplication facts onto tape immediately after learning them, and then to listen to the tape on other occasions. Get the children to use a Dictaphone when recording information from books or when working outside to record their thoughts. It is a good idea to use an LSA in these instances to help the child to do this.

In order to see the difficulties and pitfalls these children face, we must try to put ourselves in their shoes and realise how frustrating life must be for them. We take our memories for granted and can concentrate without thinking, but many children cannot, and need to be taught ways that will benefit them long-term. Both teachers and children require, above all, patience and time until significant changes occur.

CHAPTER FIVE

## LITERACY SKILLS

Literacy skills are a vital part of our daily lives and it is worrying to know how many children leave school with low levels of achievement in this area. Language-impaired children often have very low levels of attainment and find reading and writing terribly difficult. This is not to say that they are incapable of doing well - quite the reverse. With the right level of support and time, many of them can achieve far more than might be expected. One of the main reasons for some language-impaired children failing is that their spoken language skills have not developed at the usual rate, and consequently they fall behind in other areas. Check their records to find out when they learned to talk, and you will probably find they were much older than the average. It is inevitable therefore that they will find reading and writing more difficult.

Children with special educational needs frequently find that writing is a laborious and difficult process which can be extremely demoralising. The problem is that this can become a vicious circle and they start believing that they cannot write. An important way of encouraging writing is to allow the children to write about subjects that interest them and fire their imaginations. For both fiction and non-fiction writing provide the children with dictionaries, word lists and thesauri to aid their writing. There are many simplified versions of these available, and encouraging their use from an early age helps children to realise they have other tools available. A word list provided with specific vocabulary will help them when writing, as they will not have to search their memories and distract themselves from the task in hand.

With the implementation of the Primary Literacy Framework, drama, speaking and listening are once again included within the learning objectives. The learning objectives are included within the strands Speaking, Listening and Responding, Group discussion, interaction, and Drama. It is important to maximise the opportunities you offer your children for these areas when planning your literacy sessions. Reading and writing are essential skills, but if a child cannot communicate effectively then their world is very limited. In this chapter I shall outline methods which you can use to help to develop literacy skills through reading, writing, speaking and listening.

## READING

During my teaching time with language-impaired children I discovered that it is easy to demoralise them when they are reading. As their skills are delayed, you may find that reading schemes have the right word level for them but the content is too young for them. There is nothing worse for a child who is already aware of their difficulties, and other children will pick up on this too. Choosing suitable material to fire them up is essential. For younger readers the Oxford Reading Tree and associated Oxford Literacy Web materials are very useful, as there are materials to reinforce the level the children are on rather than moving them on too quickly. This enables them to have plenty to read without getting bored with the same text. If you are interested in real books, Badger books and reading boxes provide themed boxes of books, which are age appropriate and from a range of authors and genres. They take the best of the most recently published fiction and also have specific recommendations for boys. Some of the boxes are specifically for guided reading with the resources that are needed to accompany the books.

At the same time as reading books, you will need to concentrate on teaching the children key high frequency words. Use flash cards and word lists and make up games with them. Playing matching pairs, snap and rhyming games will make this aspect of things less tedious and far more enjoyable for you and the child.

## Reading schemes and free choice

The first aspect of reading which needs to be considered is the type of material that you provide for the children. Many schools have specific schemes which they adhere to and use throughout the year groups. It may be worth considering investing in other tandem schemes that can be used alongside the chosen one. Progress is often very slow when teaching language-impaired children to read and you may find that they are not ready to move on to the next level of books, even though they have read them all. You need to find other material to support the vocabulary that has been taught, and reinforce their learning without them having to re-read books. It is not a negative step, merely a way of establishing a very solid understanding and knowledge of essential vocabulary. If you rush children through a scheme too quickly, then they will soon become disheartened as the ability level increases. You can still help them to feel a real sense of achievement by allowing them to think they have completed a stage although they are continuing to work on a parallel scheme. Use stickers and star charts to encourage them, as this always has a beneficial effect and helps them to feel in control of what they are learning. Using a reading diary to record the titles and authors of the books they read is also important. They can fill in the information about the books themselves, taking information from the book and transferring it to the relevant part of their diary. They can then look back on what they have read over a period of time and feel a real sense of achievement.

Another way of generating enthusiasm for reading is to allow children to choose a book which is not from an official reading scheme. Free choice does not mean that they have free rein in the library choosing something wholly unsuitable. Provide a selection of books to choose from. Offer different types of text, short stories, poetry and plays to maintain interest. These texts can be read alongside scheme books to give a bit of variety and a feeling that they are not just on scheme books, which can ultimately become a disincentive.

# Non-fiction

Reading non-fiction can be a great way to encourage children to read with interest and enthusiasm. They are often keener to read about a hobby or something they are interested in, and it can be a welcome change from fiction. Non-fiction texts have short captions and labelled diagrams, which may be far less daunting to read than a whole page of text. The illustrations and diagrams also give visual clues as to the content of the text and can add to the value of the reading experience.

The school library is a vital and useful resource from which to search for books on chosen subjects. Using the various means available to locate books on certain subjects also entails reading, but the children are unaware of this. They can gain confidence by successfully looking for and finding a book they wish to read. If you can, give them time with another more able reader or an adult helper to explore the library. They will be able to see how they can use it as a valuable resource, even though they may not be the most capable reader. Allowing these children to have access to real books is vital, otherwise they can feel shut out from a whole world which others can attain by reading well. You need to make them feel that books are for everyone, not just able readers.

# Paired or shared reading

Paired reading involves sitting with a partner and reading a book together. Reading together or taking it in turns to read a page or a paragraph can boost their confidence and enable them to read more happily. In this way they can start to read material that they would not normally have a chance to read. If children are really under-confident or are desperate to read a book that is inappropriate, then try reading a paragraph or page to them while they follow the text and then get them to read it back to you afterwards. They will start following the text and scanning the page and will hear the sounds of words as they see them. This will have a beneficial effect on them as their skills develop. It is not necessarily something you should do as a matter of course, but it can boost their self-esteem more than you would expect. Use it as a bargaining point for each time they complete a book, and make it a special occasion. Reading with another child can also be a good way of improving self-esteem, provided you choose their partner carefully. Children can be very sensitive and perceptive, and reading with one of their peers could be far less daunting than reading to an adult. Literacy sessions provide valuable opportunities for this to take place without the children necessarily realising the roles they are playing.

# Reading comprehension

One of the most important aspects of reading is the child's understanding of what they have read. There is no point in developing children's sight vocabulary if they have no understanding of what they have read. You must ensure that you spend time questioning them about what they have just read immediately afterwards. You can extend this when they are about to read again by asking them to recall what they read last time. They can begin to predict what happens next and compare their predictions with the actual events. The comprehension questions need to be a mixture of closed and open so that the children have to think more carefully about the text. For example, 'What is the name of the dog in the story?', 'How do you think the dog's owner felt when the dog ran away?'. The aim is to give them opportunities to formulate their own ideas and make assumptions about the text.

# Reading goals

For children who have difficulty motivating themselves, it is a good idea to set them goals and targets for their reading. These targets could be very simple, such as, read one new book a week or read to someone at home at least four times a week. Once these goals are being reached, the children should be rewarded in some way, by using stickers and certificates for example. As the children become more confident readers, your goals can become more difficult. For example, read two books about insects or draw your own book cover for the book you have just read. The goals do not need to be long and complicated, but enough to give them an incentive to work towards. If reading could be a precursor to an activity they enjoy related to the book, then you may find you have even more success.

# Book reviews

Writing a book review may sound fairly dull, but it can be made into a more exciting and enjoyable activity. Book reviews need not be a straightforward piece of writing about a book. Try to create a display by writing the name and title of the book on a shaped piece of paper such as a leaf and attaching it to a tree, or cloud shapes on a landscape. For those who find writing more difficult, ask them to choose two words to describe the book and write them on the shape too. They are still able to get their opinion across about the book without struggling with writing. This can be extended into a sentence as they become more confident. The review could also be written up in a picture form with speech bubbles, briefly outlining some of the good and bad points about the book. Similarly you could divide a page in half with a smiley face on one side and a sad face on the other and they could write a list of good and bad points. However you decide to do this, it is important that you provide somewhere for these reviews to be made available to all the children, so a file or folder should be filled with their work. Other children can then read the reviews and it may help them to decide what they wish to read. It is important to remember that you must do this with reading scheme books as well as non-scheme books.

# WRITING FICTION

Story writing is a difficult skill for any child with language difficulties in whatever shape or form, as many find the effort of imagining and then recording a story almost impossible. One or the other may be achieved, but neither with a huge amount of success. There are ways of getting the process started more easily. Many of the following ideas are good starting points for developing writing further in the future. The basic ideas can be adapted for other subjects or purposes, but these are particularly useful when writing fiction.

## Cartoon Strips

Divide up a piece of paper into four or six sections and get the children to work out the main parts of the story to fit in these spaces. They can then illustrate the story and write a short sentence or two beneath. Similarly, children can write captions related to illustrations and pictures when writing non-fiction. They can go on to use these cartoon strips to develop a longer piece of writing, which could be used as a planning mechanism for a story or a storyboard for a play or a puppet show. The possibilities are endless and you will find that most children in the class will enjoy writing in this way. They could use this as a means of starting to write a proper book and can test out their ideas on other people. You may well find that, despite this being such a simple idea, you can get some good quality writing, which is well structured. Writing in this way concentrates the mind on what is being written and how the story will be divided up. It is a clear visual plan as well as a legitimate written format.

## Speech Bubbles

To start with, it would be a good idea to show the children a picture of two people or characters who look as if they could be talking to each other. Ask them what might be going on in the picture, what has happened before and after and what might be being said. Once they have discussed this, ask them to go away and write what each character is thinking or saying. Use examples from real comics to illustrate this, as it can be quite difficult to understand how to write them without seeing an example.

Instead of expecting children to write longer sentences for the cartoon strips mentioned above, they could write the story as speech bubbles. The writing is then concise and the children are focussed on what is happening in the pictures. It means they have to think about the verbal responses people make when in conversation or after a question has been asked. Using conversation to prepare this work would be a good idea, in other words ask them to talk you through their pictures and then record this. Brevity is important, but the writing must make sense.

## Pictures

Using pictures as a focal point for story writing can really help children to get started. It takes away some of the pressure of trying to imagine a story or create ideas from nothing. Even if you have given them a good introduction and starting point for a story, children can still find it very daunting to have to launch into their own words.

If you would like the children to re-tell a known story, find copies of simple pictures from an existing text. If you are able to, photocopy the pictures and mix them up so the children need to think about the ordering of the events. Ask them to sequence the pictures correctly and then re-tell the story out loud. Once they have done this confidently, ask them to write the story using the pictures as a prompt. You could help by recording some of the vocabulary they used on a piece of paper or even recording their oral version on tape. By playing the tape back, they can record on paper what they have said and lessen the fear of committing themselves in black and white.

Another way of helping would be to provide a selection of pictures of people, places and events taken from magazines and newspapers and ask the children to select a few. The pictures can then be used to start a story and give help with describing characters and settings. Any of these techniques should help you to get a more positive response to writing, as the children do not have to concentrate on so many different things at the same time. Writing in itself is hard enough, without having to be imaginative and retain information at the same time.

## Limit the number of sentences to be written

One of the most daunting things about writing for children with specific special needs is the sheer scale of the task ahead of them. As was mentioned above, give them starting points and goals to help them to complete a task successfully. Tell them how many sentences they need to write in order to complete the task, for example, two sentences to introduce the characters, three to tell the main part of the story and one to conclude. They could use counters to work out how many sentences they have completed and the task will not seem so onerous. Similarly if they are working with an LSA they can tell the story out loud then write one sentence themselves, then the LSA the next, continuing to alternate. You should not expect language-impaired children to complete the amount of work the average child can produce. They have hurdles to overcome, not least of which is their confidence. You can destroy any steps you have made by diminishing what they have achieved, however small. This is not to say that you should automatically have low expectations of these children, more that you should be realistic about what they can achieve and improve this little by little.

## Story plans

When you want children to begin to write stories they need some sort of starting point to help them to organise their thoughts and ideas. A good way of doing this is to give them a pre-prepared story plan which they can fill in. This should include headings such as characters, setting, beginning, middle (event one, two and so on) and ending. By talking through the way in which a story is structured and completing a plan, writers should be able to create an exciting piece of fiction. Without preparation, many children would automatically jump straight into the middle of the story without considering the events that lead up to the major events, or even what will happen at the end. You should spend at least a whole session planning a story in order to do this real justice, and you may not even get as far as writing the actual story. This does not matter, as the planning of a story is the most critical point of the process.

## WRITING NON-FICTION

Writing non-fiction can often be a simpler process for children with language difficulties. It generally requires no imagination and they have the facts to hand, so the effort is purely in the physical aspect of writing. This simplifies many parts of the writing process, as children do not have to use an extensive imaginative vocabulary or write about something that does not exist. Using their experiences is easier to record and the results are generally more successful. The following are suggestions of ways in which you can enhance the process of non-fiction writing.

## Dictaphones

When carrying out scientific experiments, it is helpful for children to talk into a Dictaphone to record what is happening as they watch. They are recording the present, which will help with their recall of events later on. The recording can be carried out in stages, which will help with organising their information. For example, they can record the equipment they collect and how they use it. Then they can talk about what they are doing, followed by the results and any conclusions they draw from it. They can listen to and use their recording to write up the information at a later date. It can help children to remember the salient points more easily and it will also help them to sequence their writing. Working with another adult or child would make this process even simpler. Dictaphones are an invaluable resource for children who have memory difficulties, or for whom remembering and writing at the same time are too much to cope with.

## Word lists

Writing fiction generally entails remembering to use adjectives and adverbs, whereas non-fiction vocabulary is very different and more specific to a topic. If you provide children with vocabulary lists specific to the topic, these will help to direct their thoughts and prevent them from worrying about the spelling of individual words, and they will find it easier to record their work. They can then concentrate on the bare bones of their writing, a far more important process than the correct spelling of more complex words.

If you would like the children to write about something, such as the school grounds, take them out with clipboards and Dictaphones. You will need to ask them to note down individual words that occur to them as they walk. After doing this, it is a good idea to get them to record their words in the form of glossaries or categorise them into types of words. Typing these up on the computer and presenting them in an interesting way can be very effective. Displaying these words in the classroom will help to reinforce their learning.

## Writing frames

As with the story plans, providing a framework can be a very successful way of enabling children to produce a good piece of non-fiction writing. The chronology of an experiment or investigation can be very difficult to remember, so providing headings alleviates some of these difficulties. The aim is that ultimately they will become used to writing in a chronological and organised way. By helping them to organise their writing in this way, children will be able to concentrate solely on writing clear and concise sentences.

## Word Processing

All children like their work to look good, and using the word processor to write their piece is an ideal way to achieve this. There are so many ways of changing the look of a bit of writing, and it will give them a real boost to see their writing look professional. You could type in the frameworks before the children start to work so they have some guidelines to follow.

## Diaries

Some schools allow children to come into the classroom before lessons officially begin, and keeping them busy is important. In order to keep them occupied in a productive way, they could have a small exercise book to write as a diary in the morning. This diary could be a book in which there is no pressure to spell correctly or write in a specific way. Many children find this an ideal way to record their thoughts freely and with more confidence.

## Non-fiction page

Most children like to produce work that is visually pleasing and interesting to look at. You could get out books from the library on your chosen topic and look at them carefully with the children. Show them examples of layout and presentation from this selection of books and talk about these important elements. The children do not necessarily need to write much, but they can concentrate on headings, sub-headings, captions and so on. This sort of work can enable them to produce a professional and exciting piece of work with the minimum amount of writing.

## Flow Charts

A scientific experiment can be written successfully, and often more effectively, as a flow-chart. In this way the children are focussing on the key elements of the task and their chronological order rather than writing long sentences about what they have done. This can be visually interesting to look at and enjoyable to read.

## Poetry

A large number of children enjoy writing poetry and have far more success with this than any other form of writing. There are many forms of poetry with rigid rules and forms that they find easier to write, for example, acrostics or haiku. It is a great way to enable children with language difficulties to enjoy a greater degree of success.

## SPEAKING AND LISTENING

The importance of speaking and listening opportunities within the classroom cannot be stressed too highly. With the implementation of the Primary Literacy Framework their importance has been raised again. Many of the social skills ideas will help to cover this aspect of their learning but it is excellent news that the Literacy curriculum recognises their importance once more.

## Small group discussion

There are many chances within the school day and curriculum when you can plan for small group discussions. Within literacy and numeracy group sessions you will inevitably need some time to talk with the children. It is important to allow every child to have a turn to speak and share with the group. For some language-impaired children, small groups are the only places where they feel confident to speak up and join in. It is important to impress on the children that everyone's contribution is valuable and worth listening to. Each individual looks at something from their own perspective, and they may find another child's ideas or suggestions can open their minds to other things too.

Other times for small group discussions that may well be overlooked are within PE sessions when children are working on a dance together, or in music when doing a group composition for example. If you think back to a typical day and remember when the children were talking together, think about whether or not this was planned for and, if not, how that opportunity could be improved in the future.

Unplanned discussions are also vital. For example, at the beginning of the school day you can chat informally with the children as they arrive. It could be about somewhere they have visited as a class, a place someone likes to visit, a television programme or even the toys they are playing with at home. Making yourself available to the children as a person who is interested in them, as well as being their teacher, can help their self-esteem.

If you set up times for the children to discuss an issue which concerns them, for example stranger awareness, then you need to think carefully about how the group will work: are some characters very dominant within the group, who may not join in and are the children going to remain on task? For younger children it may well be an idea to provide a list of questions that they could consider within the topic and focus their attention more specifically. Their discussion is likely to be more meaningful and focussed if you do this and they will get more out of it. Within this kind of session it may also be an idea to nominate a chairman who is effectively in control of the discussion. Their role is to ensure that everyone has a turn and is given the opportunity to put their own point across rather than being shouted down.

## Role-play and drama

Role-play and drama have already been mentioned within the social skills chapter. It is worth noting here, however, that role-play can be brought into many aspects of the classroom curriculum. It is a useful tool within literacy sessions when you wish to work on a piece of text the children have been reading; in history it is an excellent way of enabling them to transport themselves into other people's lives.

## Speaking cards

The use of cards with a question mark has already been mentioned in an earlier chapter, and this technique could be employed with speaking cards. If you are having trouble with children who speak up too little or too often, make a set of cards with some symbol on to represent speech. These could be distributed to certain individuals so that they know that you expect them to participate in a discussion. You could give a child with verbal diarrhoea just one card so they know they may only speak once, therefore getting them to think carefully about what they say and when they say it. For a child with a lack of confidence you could give them three cards, so they are expecting to have to speak more often and they know you will facilitate that.

## Presentations

A fun way to encourage children to speak up is to have a spot a couple of times a week where the children take it in turns to prepare a mini-presentation on a subject of their choice. It can be an activity they enjoy out of school, information about a place they visited or anything they like. It gives them a forum to bring in a little piece of themselves to share with the class. At the end of each presentation allow the others the chance to ask a limited number of questions. This means that the presenter has to think on their feet a little as well. These need not be long-winded sessions; you can set a variable time limit according to the individual speaking, but they will hopefully feel that they have something of value to contribute to the class.

Teaching literacy skills need not be dry and boring. By varying the ways in which you teach them, your lessons will be more exciting and the children will make far more progress. From these ideas it can be seen that all kinds of writing can be fun and can be presented to the children in many different, imaginative ways. Many of these suggestions can be modified and adapted to specific circumstances and topics, but should enable children with language difficulties to produce written work they can be proud of. These ideas can be used to promote reading and writing with the rest of the children as well but the most important thing to remember is that children with difficulties need their confidence developed by slightly adapting your expectations and gradually building up their stamina. Expecting them to read for a long time or write pages and pages is going to have a detrimental effect on them.

A classroom where children's reading and writing is valued and important is a classroom where the children are motivated and enjoy learning. Whatever they are able to achieve should always be celebrated and encouraged, and the rest of the class should be made aware of their steps towards success. Finally, by displaying their written work in the classroom or in the form of a class book can do wonders for children's self-esteem and will give them the impetus to produce work of a high standard in the future.

CHAPTER SIX

# MATHEMATICS

Teaching mathematics skills to a class of children can be challenging at the best of times, as children learn at different rates and in different ways. A child with a language impairment is no more or less likely to struggle with mathematical concepts than any other child. As with most lessons, their biggest stumbling block is usually with the language. Provided you are consistent with your use of vocabulary and use simple sentences that are clear and concise, a child with a flair for mathematics should have few problems. However, there are children (and obviously not just those with language impairment) who will have greater difficulties, and there are a variety of tactics that you could use to make these lessons more valuable learning experiences.

## The Role of the LSA

Your LSA will have a vital role to play within mathematics sessions. First of all, it is important that she sits beside the child or children who have difficulties and helps to focus their attention on what is being said during your formal teaching. Once they move from the whole class teaching part of the lesson, her role is even more vital. The children will possibly need someone to help them to organise themselves, ensuring they have the right books, writing materials and equipment if necessary. The amount of time that can be wasted by not knowing which book to record their work in is astonishing. Use the trigger cards mentioned in *Chapter 2* to give them a visual prompt as to what they need before they start the mathematical task, and their preparation time will be shorter.

Once the children have everything they need to start their work, then the LSA should help them to read the question they have to answer and talk through what it means with the child. This will involve discussing the vocabulary and talking to the child about what they are being asked to do. Sometimes all that is needed is to rephrase the question in such a way that the child understands, or to break up the question into manageable chunks of information.

With a greater emphasis on problem solving in mathematics, written language is used far more. During SATs children with specific difficulties usually lose confidence when faced with a written question or instructions rather than with numerical problems. Textbooks usually have a lot of information printed on the page. This has to be read and understood before a task can be carried out and the LSA needs to step in at this point. It is vital not to underestimate the importance of this role. Often the fact that someone else has read out the question to them means that the children are able to go ahead and tackle the mathematics with confidence. Because reading can affect what the children achieve, you must take care when assessing their ability. Their innate mathematical ability may not be obvious, purely because they struggle to comprehend the way problems are presented to them.

An adult working nearby or alongside a child with difficulties can help to motivate them to start an activity and give them the incentive to continue when they find things tough. Children should have the confidence to feel they can ask the LSA to check through the initial work they do. In this way they are able to be sure that they are doing the right thing and the LSA can ensure that they have internalised the method of working out and are not repeating errors consistently.

One further way your LSA can be used is to supply number facts if necessary. If you have been teaching the children about data handling, for example, your objective may not necessarily be for them to recall all their number facts accurately. In this instance, it is of more importance that the children are able to complete a chart and derive information from it, and not to be able to make accurate calculations. Give the children a list of basic number facts that they can use as a reference, or ask the LSA to supply them with this information. The children can then maintain the momentum of the task without getting caught up in additional mathematical workings which are not critical to the aims of the lesson.

## Small group support

When teaching mathematics it is important to be able to teach within small groups as well as whole class sessions. This is not just important for children with a form of learning disability, but for all abilities. Some children face difficulties when listening in large groups for sustained periods of time. This can have a real impact on how much information they can attend to and retain. The language barrier for some children can really hinder their ability to comprehend what is being taught, let alone put it into practice afterwards. As with any lesson, it is a good idea to keep these children behind for a moment or two to ask them to repeat back to you what they have to do. With maths you could work through a couple of examples with them separately so that you have more confidence that they understand the lesson. Many children will say they understand for an easy life, and will then go to their place and spend most of their working time getting ready to start without achieving anything. This is not necessarily just time-wasting, it could merely be because they did not understand. Spending time with them before they start their task could eradicate many of these problems. You will discover where their misconceptions lie and where the fundamental problems occur. You can then teach them on a smaller, more individual, basis with more emphasis on their specific difficulties. This role can be taken over by an LSA when the topic is not entirely new. Working with small groups can really help you to identify specific weaknesses in their understanding and hopefully these can be addressed before they become too entrenched in the children's minds.

## Small steps

It is important when you are teaching new mathematical concepts that you try to teach in small steps, gradually introducing new stages slowly and at a gradual pace, so that the children are able to practise and consolidate their new skills. Once they have mastered the basic concept, then introduce the next stage in their learning. This is equally important when you revisit a topic which has been previously taught. You must ensure that the children's basic knowledge is secure before moving on to the next stage.

## Number lines

Number lines are extremely useful when teaching mathematics. There are a number of different styles and sizes available to schools, and they are vital when aiding children with some form of learning difficulty. Display large-scale number lines in the classroom which can be used as visual aids during whole class sessions. At the same time, it would be helpful to give specific children a small copy of the line which they can touch and follow directly.

It is useful to laminate number lines and use overhead projector pens to write on them. In this way the children can mark directly on the line as they work through calculations, and have greater confidence that their answer is correct. When teaching small groups, use these lines so that every child is working out each question, rather than one individual answering. In this way they are practising their numeracy skills without necessarily being the child in the spotlight.

Provide the children with a selection of different number lines, for example 0-10, 0-100 and lines where the numbers do not necessarily jump one at a time. In this way they have to think about what is missing.

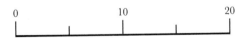

Ask them to fill in the gaps on a line, not necessarily from the beginning. Ask them to start in the middle of a line or from the end going backwards. With practice, the children should become more familiar with the ordering of numbers and their relationship with one another.

Some children find it helpful to have a complete number line stuck permanently onto the desk in front of them. As their confidence increases, you can change the line by removing numbers but leaving the demarcations where they were, then just leaving a few specific numbers along the line.

## Recording

One thing that can hamper a child's learning when they have a language difficulty is having to record information. If they can concentrate on the core skills they are learning without having to worry about how they are going to write it down, then the lesson may well be more successful all round. They should retain more of the work they are doing and would be able to remember the processes they are practising.

It would be a good idea to provide children with a format they can copy or fill in so that they have fewer problems with recording. When starting a new topic, it would be a good idea to put examples up on a board so the whole class can see. This is important for both numerical sentences and written answers, for example:

$$4 \times 5 = 20$$
Four sets of five make twenty.
The tallest child is Thomas.

By showing them examples or by writing them up so the children can see the way things can be recorded, they will have more confidence when they need to write their own work. This means that when they return to the same topic next time, they should have a better idea about how to record their work. The other thing that would be of use would be to write their work into their books for them. This can be done either by you or an LSA.

## Questioning

Your questioning of the children during teaching sessions is critical to the way in which they learn or respond to your teaching. By asking questions that encourage them to take an active part in the lesson, or asking questions that will stretch them, you can influence the way in which they learn. Closed questions can have a limited role within discussion sessions or lessons in which you wish the children to think laterally. However, within maths sessions the children often need to give a definitive answer to a question. Simplify your language when asking these questions and try not to use too much vocabulary that complicates things. It is important to enable the children to focus on the mathematical aspect of the process they are learning and being asked about. With too much language within the question they can easily lose the thread of what you are asking and consequently lose interest or become confused. This kind of questioning is particularly important at the start of a new topic when the children are beginning to learn and take new ideas on board.

Once they are more confident and have more firmly established ideas, then the children can be questioned slightly differently. For example, before the beginning of the next session ask them what they learned the day before and test their memory by working through a couple of examples with them. See if they explain to you what to do, rather than you doing the work. Involve the children in adding to or refining these explanations as they are doing this.

Try to ask more open questions once the children are a little more confident with what they have learned. Try to place more of an emphasis on problem solving and putting the mathematics in a realistic context. It is essential that the children should see how what they are learning is relevant to real life. Some topics are obviously more suited to this and easier to relate to for the children. However, it is worth trying hard to make it relevant to them without stretching credibility too far.

## Practical apparatus

Many children find it hard to comprehend mathematical calculations without using some form of practical apparatus. It is important to know when this is a useful tool and when the children are just relying on apparatus as a crutch so that they can avoid thinking for themselves. However, there are many resources which can be used to great effect when teaching mathematics. Something as simple as providing squared paper for the children to work on can make a real difference to the presentation of their work and ultimately their understanding of concepts such as place value. By organising and laying out their work in a more structured manner their thoughts will become more organised.

Most schools have multilink blocks, and these are essential when teaching basic number skills. They can provide an excellent visual aid when explaining number operations such as multiplication and division. When teaching basic addition and subtraction number facts, the children should say the facts aloud as they place cubes out in front of them. This multi-sensory approach should help them to recall the facts more easily in the future. Cuisenaire rods can also be used to help children learn these basic skills and gives them another way at looking at which numbers are bigger and smaller. Grouping and sharing cubes can help them to understand the concepts of multiplication and division. They should be used to consolidate the children's learning and help them to visualise numbers.

Multilink can also be used to great effect when teaching data handling and creating bar charts. The children can make 3D charts using the blocks before drawing a chart on paper. This will help them to make statements about the data, as they may find it easier to work out the highest and lowest quantities from the apparatus. It adds another dimension to their learning and increases their understanding of certain processes.

When carrying out measuring work it is vital to ensure that the children have access to a wide range of practical equipment. They will learn more by actively weighing, measuring and investigating for themselves. Independent recording is not so vital in some sessions; completing mathematical investigations and understanding the processes is far more important. It is possible to adapt some lessons so that the class is directly active and involved as a whole when, for example, making human bar charts or weighing each other and classroom equipment. Use your imagination to make your lessons as exciting as possible with plenty of active participation. The children will learn more from doing, rather than sitting and listening all the time.

## Word lists

At the beginning of every new mathematical topic it is important to spend some time going over the vocabulary and ensuring the children are secure with their understanding of the meaning of each word. It would be particularly useful to print up a large list to be displayed in the classroom so the children can refer to it as they work. It is important at this stage to ensure that if there are two words for the same thing, such as divide and share, that the children should be familiar and confident with each word. Children with language difficulties should be given their own copy of each word list and keep them filed for future reference. The words can be brought out whenever necessary and added to as they progress. If you feel it is appropriate, it would be a good idea to send a copy of the words home with the children so that they can familiarise themselves with them. It may have an effect on their confidence during lesson times if they are hearing and using the words at home as well. At the same time, their parents are aware of what they are learning in school and can support them from home.

Another way of improving the use and understanding of mathematical vocabulary is to ensure that the children talk through their work. In this way they are using the words in context. By saying the words and doing the calculations at the same time, their meaning should become clearer and more embedded in the children's memories. Ensure that you use all the different words that mean the same thing while teaching and talking so that they become used to hearing them all the time.

## Dictaphones

The use of Dictaphones has already been mentioned in connection with literacy and general curriculum use. Their use in helping children to recall and learn basic number facts is also important. Times tables and basic addition and subtraction number facts can be read into the Dictaphone by the child and played back as and when necessary. The act of saying the facts aloud and recording them in their own voice should help them to learn more easily. Listening back to the recording to check that it is accurate is very important.

After this, they can use the tape as a memory jogger, to listen to in the car on the way to the shops, as a revision tool or simply to double-check work they have completed. The tape can be added to as their learning develops and you can decide on the next facts to be learned between you.

Another use for a Dictaphone could be when trying to solve a question. Ask the child to read the question into the machine and then listen back to it, as many times as is necessary to help them to make sense of what they have to do.

SATs place an emphasis on answering oral mental maths questions, and this can be very daunting for the language-impaired child. Start practising with a recording of your voice asking mental maths problems and get the child used to listening to a familiar voice before the actual assessment. This could also be a real help to many other members of the class, but these children could take a tape home, listen to it in more relaxed surroundings and start becoming more comfortable with the idea. They can stop the tape and take as long as they need to answer to begin with, and then build up the speed of their answers as their confidence increases.

## Games

Playing games can help to make mathematics more comprehensible and enjoyable for children. Use games to reinforce basic concepts once the children have completed their initial work. There are many ready-made board games available, which you can buy from high-street shops or specialist educational suppliers. Another way of using games is to make your own card games from blank packs. There are text books available which give you ideas about games you can make, but the simplest game you can make is to write a number up to 20 (or whatever you are working on) on each card and shuffle them. In another pile, make cards with different mathematical symbols (+, −, × and ÷) and their word equivalents (add, plus, more than, subtract, minus, take away, less than, difference, multiply, times, lots of, divide and share). The children need to turn over two number cards and one symbol card and then calculate the sum. They get one point if their answer is correct and two if they can make a second sum using the numbers, for example:

$$4x5 = 20$$
$$5+5+5+5 = 20$$
$$18 \text{ divided by } 3 = 6$$
$$6 \text{ sets of } 3 = 18$$

Playing verbal games to test children's basic number fact knowledge is also good fun. You could put them into teams and give them a bell or a buzzer to press when they know the answer. The most important thing is to make learning fun and give them a sense of achievement.

## Colour-coded Keywords

Colour coding was mentioned in an earlier chapter and the same applies to mathematics. When working on a new topic, colour code the keywords you are going to use. For example, addition words could be red and subtraction words blue. In this way the children can begin to establish a more confident approach to their learning in each session. They will begin to recognise the operation needed by the colour and eventually this will help them to remember the exact meaning of each word.

## Simplify Text Books

Some mathematical textbooks have very long-winded explanations at the beginning of each chapter or new section, and this can be very daunting. As has been said, the children are learning mathematical concepts, not how to read, and it is important to allow them the opportunity to complete work successfully without panicking about the words on a page. Check through the books before the lesson and see if you can adapt the text to suit the children. It may mean some photocopying and cutting and pasting, but this can be used as a resource for the whole school.

## Repetition

When you are teaching, it is really frustrating to ask a question and to get no reply. Some children need to process the information presented to them more slowly and are not necessarily unable to answer. If this is the case, do not be tempted to ask the question in a different way with different words. Repeat your question using the same words, otherwise the children have to start processing your verbal information all over again and this will delay the answer further. If they continue to have difficulty interpreting what you are saying, talk through your question slowly and ask them what kind of mathematics they are being asked to do. Then ask them to repeat the figures they need to use, so that they are hearing what you have asked, but this has been broken down into manageable and understandable chunks.

## Paired or small group work

Pairing the children up or working with a very small group on the same task can be highly successful. It gives the children more confidence and they may achieve far more as a result. Many language-impaired children have good mathematical abilities; it is just the comprehension of the language surrounding it that causes the problems. By working with a partner, they may be able to complete their work without too much teacher intervention. Once they have talked through what they have been asked to do, the mathematics may seem more straightforward. A partner can help with the accurate and logical recording of a task as well.

## Hierarchies

The use of hierarchies of words was mentioned in *Chapter 2*. Mathematical terms can be placed in hierarchies too. It could be something straightforward, like terms used for weight and mass or the properties of triangles. For example:

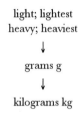

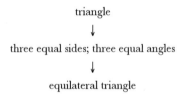

By doing this, it means that the children will gradually learn vocabulary in a controlled and organised manner, adding information to their memories a little at a time.

## Deconstructing questions

Written questions are often overly complex or obscure at first sight to children with language difficulties. You will need to teach them how to deconstruct questions in order to understand them. The first stage is to read through the question aloud. Once they have done this, read through again and then find the question words. Highlight these words in a colour so they are obvious. The next stage is to find the most important information within the question and highlight this in another colour. After that, read through the question one more time and cross out any unnecessary words, for example:

> ~~The teacher went to the store cupboard and found some new pencils.~~
> ~~She gave them to the~~ 30 children ~~in the classroom. They had~~ 6 pencils
> each ~~and there were~~ 5 left over. **How many** pencils did the teacher collect?

This ensures that the child will have read the question through several times and will have absorbed the information more readily. When looking back at the question, the important information will be more obvious. By practising this technique frequently, the children will begin to learn how to find the relevant information within a set of words.

## Class puzzle

Try to inspire the children to enjoy mathematics by having an area of the classroom where there is equipment set up each week with some form of problem to be solved. This could either be related to the current class topic if you so wish, or something completely separate. The children could be given opportunities to attempt this before school, for example at playtimes, or when they have a few spare minutes after completing a task. It could have an element of competition and there could be a box beside it where the children could post their solutions. The puzzle or problem should be as open-ended as possible so the children can find their own way of tackling it. Leave out everything they could need for the task, including writing materials, so there is no need to organise themselves to start the task. It may be helpful to set the problem out in stages so that higher ability mathematicians can stretch themselves further and others can achieve at their own level.

These techniques should help you to support language-impaired children within your classroom more successfully. Mathematics sessions should be less difficult for them, and they may find they are able to contribute more confidently both within small groups and with the whole class.

CHAPTER SEVEN

# GENERAL CURRICULUM SUPPORT

It is not just within literacy and numeracy sessions that language-impaired children face daily difficulties. When you look closely at the attainment targets for the foundation subjects, it is obvious that language and communication skills play a large part in the curriculum. It is essential to plan for these within every subject and be aware of the difficulties the children will face. In this chapter support and strategies for each subject will be offered, with particular emphasis on the specific language aspects of the attainment targets.

## SCIENCE

Many of the strategies that have been outlined for the other curriculum subjects can be used or adapted for science. The children will need to talk to others as well as explain their work to you during these sessions, and you need to plan carefully for these occasions. The children need to describe things they observe or predict within all aspects of science, and on top of this they will need to learn specific vocabulary according to the particular topic they are working on. Vocabulary lists are essential and the idea of hierarchical language mentioned in *Chapters 2 and 6* is very necessary. For example:

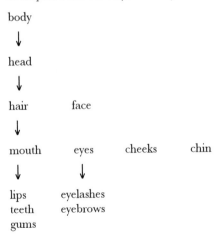

If you teach the necessary vocabulary in this way, then the children will gradually be able to build up a word bank in their memories, with time to recall and retain each new word as they learn it. Throwing all the words at them in one go will only confuse them and they will retain little or nothing. By teaching in this way, they should be able to make more sense of the subject they are learning about.

If you use prepared formats for children to fill in as they investigate and conduct experiments, this will enable them to concentrate on the subject matter, rather than on how they are going to present the information at the end. It gives them a framework and a structure on which they can record their work in a simple and easily-read format. This means that when they revisit a topic they can recall what they were doing far more readily. The examples below may give you some ideas as to how you can enable them to present their work in a more independent manner.

| Items which are attracted to a magnet | Items which are not attracted to a magnet |
|---|---|
|  |  |

| Things which I think will float | Things that floated | Things which I think will sink | Things that sank |
|---|---|---|---|
|  |  |  |  |

It may seem very simplistic, but giving children this sort of assistance will enable them to record their ideas and observations without the unnecessary chore of planning their method of recording. They can do the activity and consider what they think will happen, observe what actually happens and fill in the chart without needing to use sentences or explanations.

Similarly, you can provide a prepared format to record more detailed information about scientific experiments when you need children to be more formal. Give them the basic headings so that they are guided through the experiment in stages and can record their work a little at a time.

---

## Scientific Investigation

Equipment I will need
What I am trying to find out

What I think will happen

What I did first
Next
Finally
What happened

I think this happened because

---

Another good way of getting them to record an investigation is to draw a flow chart sequencing their actions and the results, using minimal vocabulary to label the drawings.

Listening to the children as they work and jotting down what they say is another way of assessing their understanding and knowledge of the subject. They could also use a Dictaphone to talk into as they work, explaining what they are using and what is happening.

# DESIGN AND TECHNOLOGY

Design and technology sessions inevitably involve a fair amount of discussion, for example when working in pairs or groups, requesting tools or materials and commenting about what is happening. Even an exclamation of frustration or despair is to a degree some form of response to the task the child is carrying out. The attainment targets include asking the children to describe and explain what they are doing and to clarify how they have come up with an idea and what it should do. The communication skills required by this subject do not rely entirely on words; mention is made of labelled sketches and models to pass on ideas to another person. This does relieve children of some of the burden, but language still plays a vital role in their ability to achieve.

One of the targets asks that the children name the tools they use so, as with the word lists for other subjects, give them a pictorial dictionary of tools so they can match the words and pictures. It has been mentioned before that labelling drawers and equipment around the classroom can really help the children, and it is equally important that they know where they can find a method of identifying something. The technology equipment should be labelled and the correct names of the tools should be used at all times by all the children.

When planning a design and technology task it would be a good idea to give the children a pre-prepared planning sheet on which to note down their thoughts in words and/or pictures. This could be adapted to include pictures or a list of tools which the children could circle if they use them during the making process. Many children find that a practical task is an excellent vent for their imaginative skills and they are able to produce some fantastic results, but that planning and evaluating the task is much harder.

| **Planning Sheet**<br>Tools needed: | **Evaluation Sheet**<br>Tools I used: |
|---|---|
| Purpose of my design:<br><br>What my model will look like:<br><br><br><br><br><br><br>What I will do first:<br><br>Next stage:<br><br>Finally: | Did my design work?<br><br>What was successful?<br><br>What was unsuccessful?<br><br>What would I do next time?<br><br>What my model looks like: |

Giving the children a framework like this does not mean that they are thinking about the task any less or that it is making it too easy for them. If anything, it allows children some space in which to think more carefully about what they have been asked to do, and provides some form of organisation to help to make the task more successful in the long run. It supplies a structure within which children can organise and plan their thoughts and ideas more carefully and logically. This is just an example of what you could give the children. You should adapt it to make it more suitable for the task they are doing. Over time you should see an improvement in the way they work and they will be able to tackle a task in a more sequential manner.

# ICT

In my experience of working with language-impaired children, I found that the children would use the computer whenever they had the opportunity to do so. We were lucky in that our resourced provision had small personal computers which were taken around the school and then the work was downloaded within our classroom later on. Most schools have one or two computers at most in each classroom and the time allocated per child is naturally limited. It is best to work on one short task at a time, giving the children more regular opportunities to work on the computer. Working in pairs or groups can also help as the time is shared among them. Teaching the children basic keyboard skills is very important before progressing on to word processing skills. Their inability to find their way around a keyboard can seriously hamper their use of a computer and any task can become laborious and slow as a result.

As in the other subjects, language is paramount to their learning right from level one, where the children are asked to talk about their use of ICT. At level two they need to talk about their use of ICT inside and outside school. For some children this will be a licence to talk non-stop about their computer games in great depth, but you will need to focus this talking and make it more relevant to what you are doing in school. You could give the children a list of questions to ask each other in small groups and see if there are any with similar experiences. Get them to chat more informally about what they do on the computer at home and how it compares to school, for example:

> *Do you have a computer at home?*
> *Who uses the computer the most?*
> *What is it used for? Research? Homework? Playing games? Internet?*
> *Do different members of your family use the computer for different things?*
> *How long do you get to spend on the computer?*
> *Which programs are your favourites?*
> *Do you have a favourite website? Why is this your favourite?*

This should make the children think more carefully about the use of the computer and why it is used in different contexts.

Another language aspect within the level descriptors is where the children are asked to give instructions to make things happen and then to describe what happens as a result. This means that they need to plan for something and their language has to be specific and focussed.

Using e-mail will mean that children have to use language to communicate in a written form, but unlike the way they write normally. They need to be able to send messages that are to the point and not too detailed. They may also need to respond to a message appropriately. Greetings and salutations generally follow a different pattern from that of normal letter writing, so they need to be taught how to compose a message using more informal wording. Giving them examples of messages which have been sent to and from people will give them ideas about how to start and finish a message and what sort of language is appropriate for a child, adult or a stranger they may need to e-mail. In order to make their e-mailing more relevant to their current topic, do some research on the internet and find organisations that have a relevance to what they are doing, for example, museums or supermarkets. Ask the children to send an e-mail requesting information from one of these organisations and await a response. You may need to do some research yourself to start with, and discover whether there is an educational division who might help. The other thing to remember is not to swamp the same organisation with messages. Try to find a range of places to ask for information and then the children may have more luck.

# HISTORY

One major obstacle faced by children with language impairment is their concept of time. History can therefore be a very challenging subject to teach, and it is never entirely obvious how well the children have grasped the concept of times past. The attainment targets discuss using everyday terms about the passing of time. From discussions with these children their concept of what happened yesterday, let alone last week, can be very uncertain. The language of time, for example yesterday, now, tomorrow, needs to be taught very thoroughly and should be an ongoing part of your routine with the class. In order to understand the passing of time and that things happened hundreds or thousands of years ago, their knowledge of the present needs to be very secure. They may well be able to tell you information about the past, but their concept of when those things actually happened may be very confused and in fact may never be completely understood. Once the children are more familiar with everyday expressions of time, then move on to teaching the language mentioned in the programmes of study, for example, a long time ago, past, ancient and modern.

Yet again, the children are expected to answer questions, give reasons for and describe events, people and changes. There is no specific mention of using appropriate and specific vocabulary beyond level 2 within the attainment targets, although the programmes of study are more specific about this. Within the programme of study it is also stated that the children are expected to communicate their findings by talking, writing and the use of ICT as with other subjects, but just be aware that whatever they produce may not show you their precise concept of the past. Using visual timelines, washing lines stretched across the classroom indicating significant moments in history, including the year/s the children were born, may help them to visualise the passing of time. For example, they may realise that there is a very small gap on the washing line between the present day and the year they were born, but that the Victorians are way back along the line, and the Romans even further.

Using pictures of the past is a good way of getting the children to talk about history. Anything they say about the buildings or the clothes people wore, for instance, is relevant and may help them to understand a little more about the changes in people's lives. Some children may understand history through one small aspect, for example, that the Romans walked, rode horses and some people used chariots to get around, whereas we walk, ride on buses, trains, aeroplanes and cars to travel around. If this very simplistic way of looking at and understanding the past is the only way they can grasp the concept, then teach them this way.

# GEOGRAPHY

Geography is a subject which also entails a great deal of discussion, inference and explanation of reasons why things happen. The children are asked to express their views on many things to do with economic and social geography, as well as the physical environment. Even at level one they are expected to ask and respond to questions about places and environments. This would obviously be at a very simple level, but could cause real problems for language-impaired children. For some, expressing a personal opinion about something could be exceptionally difficult and they would struggle to cope with having to justify and explain themselves. As an adult, think about how difficult it can be when someone challenges you after you have expressed an opinion and you have to come up with coherent and decisive reasons for your view. Sometimes, if you feel very passionately about something, it is not a problem, but at other times it can be a real struggle to be convincing, particularly if you have not thought very deeply about the issue. If you are faced with someone who has very strong arguments for the other side, it can be daunting to justify yourself. Children can feel that way in the classroom. They know you will challenge them and that you have more knowledge at your fingertips. Be aware of this and work on getting them to be confident about expressing an opinion before you tackle the reasoning. This will take time and patience, both for you and the rest of the children. Using your LSA or working with a small group yourself can help the children to feel more confident in these situations.

Within the attainment targets there is again an emphasis on the use of appropriate vocabulary. The importance of teaching vocabulary rather than just expecting the children to pick it up as they go along cannot be stressed too much. As with the other subjects, provide the children with a vocabulary list and build this up as they learn. It would help all the children if they developed glossaries of their own during each new topic so that they could refer back to them at a later date. Revision of previous work would be easier and the children would not be able to say they had not done the work before, as the evidence would be in front of them in their own writing. As a school, or a subject co-ordinator, it would be worth developing essential vocabulary lists for each year group so the teachers know what they should be concentrating on with their class.

Within the geography curriculum it may well be necessary for children to conduct some form of survey about their local area and they will need to gather evidence. It would be particularly helpful if they could work on developing questionnaires to ask local people when they are in the field. This would mean they would not have to remember the questions they need to ask, their vocabulary would be accurate and the children would also have the confidence to ask the questions as they are printed in front of them. As a consequence there is less chance of failure. Encourage the more timid children and those with a language need to be more proactive in these situations, rather than being happy to sit back and watch others.

## ART

At primary age, each level within the attainment targets requires some aspect of direct communication with the teacher or other children. It is quite possible that a child could theoretically fail to achieve a specific level of attainment purely because of the language demands imposed on them. For example at level one the children are asked to 'describe what they think or feel about their own and others' work'. This is no mean feat for a child with language difficulties, either formulating a response in terms of the language required or being able to articulate their feelings about something. The other levels involve commenting on the differences between their work and that of other children and also relate it to the context of the work they were asked to do. These are very sophisticated skills for any child to achieve and will need support to enable them to make valid and justifiable comments. One of the difficulties faced by children with semantic-pragmatic disorder, for example, is that of being far too blunt and honest, and they are capable of causing offence. Now of course this is something that any child could do, but we have to teach children how to phrase their criticism and positive comments in a more acceptable way. From experience, many of us know how hurtful it is to be told that something is 'rubbish' when we have put in a lot of effort and know that we do not have the natural talent of others. Give the children a list of phrases or words that could be used in a positive and negative context when discussing their own work and other people's. To assist those who are really struggling hard, give them a tick sheet where they can grade the work by number, for example:

---

### Art Appreciation

---

Read the questions and circle the number which best suits how you feel
(1 is poor, 5 is excellent)

How well do you feel you carried out this activity?

1      2      3      4      5

Did you use the media appropriately?

1      2      3      4      5

Did you enjoy using this media?

1      2      3      4      5

Look at someone else's work. How well do you feel they carried out this activity?

1      2      3      4      5

Do you feel they used the media appropriately?

1      2      3      4      5

---

It is important to talk to the children as they are carrying out their art activities, both at the planning stage and as they complete the work. Use the information they give you informally to help you to assess how well they are able to 'criticise' artwork. As with all other subjects, the children should be given a list of vocabulary to enable them to discuss their work appropriately.

## MUSIC

---

You may feel that music is an aspect of the curriculum where the children should have no language difficulties; in fact the reverse is the case. The level one descriptor states that the children "use their voices in different ways such as speaking, singing and chanting, and perform with awareness of others". This may at first sight not appear to be too difficult, but consider children whose language is a real handicap and to whom the thought of performing to anyone can be terrifying. They are probably all too aware of others and to speak, sing or chant in front of children, however familiar they are, is daunting.

This is asking the children to focus specifically on their voices, something many of them are desperately trying not to do. Many are so aware of their difficulties that this is placing an added pressure on them. This may sound like doom and gloom but it is the worst-case scenario. Many children relish music lessons and they can find a real release for their artistic nature. The most famous example of this is the pop singer Gareth Gates who has achieved a great deal and raised far more public awareness of speech impairments after appearing on the television programme Pop Idol.

After this initial level descriptor, there is little emphasis on language until about level four where the children are asked to respond to music using the appropriate musical vocabulary, and they are asked to evaluate their own and others' work. The children should be encouraged to respond to music in a variety of ways. This does not necessarily need to be verbal. You could give them tick sheets to show how they responded to the music, or ask them to draw a picture having listened to a piece. You can glean a great deal of information about how music makes them feel by watching their facial expression or body language.

---

### Music Appreciation

What was the music called?

Who wrote the music?

Did you like the music?      Yes        No

How did the music make you feel?
Happy        Sad          Excited        Serious        Peaceful

---

You may find that children will respond in a different way from normal when they are involved in something artistic and you may find this is an excellent way of getting to know them and discovering a way to enable them to open up.

## PE

The physical education level descriptors ask the children to use a fair amount of verbal language. At level one they are asked to describe and comment on their own and others' actions and talk about how they feel when they exercise. The language needed to explain some of these things can be quite tricky for the children to grasp, and you may find you are none the wiser as to their feelings. Teach them the appropriate language to use about their own feelings such as 'warm', 'puffed out', 'tingling', or 'exciting'. You will also need to emphasise the language you are using to comment on specific types of activity. This will obviously differ according to the type of activity, for example, balancing, dribbling or control. It is not necessary to teach this language formally, but just make sure you use the vocabulary carefully during your lessons so that the children are very aware of what they are supposed to be doing and how to verbalise it.

When the children are expected to comment on each other's performance and suggest improvements, they may encounter serious pitfalls. They can easily upset other children without realising or intending to, but they are not necessarily able to empathise with others' feelings.

## ALL CURRICULUM AREAS

Many of these ideas are interchangeable between subjects and can be adapted and personalised to suit your teaching. They should give you a starting point and a bit of assistance in providing for the children's language needs within the wider curriculum. As you spend more time with language-impaired children, you will be able to assess their needs more successfully, and you may find you need to alter your approach between subjects depending on where their natural talents lie. You may also find that some days you need to take seemingly backward steps in order to achieve a satisfactory result for you all. The most important thing to remember with these children is that you will need to adapt and change many aspects of the curriculum in order to achieve small steps, and that you will need to reinforce the work you are doing more frequently in order that they may feel secure with their language and understanding of the topic.

CHAPTER EIGHT

# HOME/SCHOOL SUPPORT AND OUTSIDE AGENCIES

Every classroom has its problems and difficulties. You may need more or less support from different quarters, even for children presenting no specific difficulties. However, working with language-impaired children will mean that you will need and receive some additional support. That support may not be continuous or particularly frequent, but when you do have access to an outside agency, use their expertise to the full to assist you with your teaching. The most likely agencies involved are speech and language therapists (SLTs), educational psychologists and occasionally occupational therapists (OTs).

## HOME/SCHOOL SUPPORT

The most important resource you have in terms of support and information are a child's parents. They can give you more background information that will enable you to plan for the child's learning more successfully. If you have a thorough understanding of the history behind a child's impairment, then you will understand the stages in learning and the rate of progression over time. If you can involve the parents as much as possible in what you are doing for their child and enable them to have opportunities to speak to you about issues as they arise, then you should be able to develop a healthy working relationship which will benefit the child.

Any small changes in the child's behaviour can be significant both at home and at school, and it is worth keeping a record of these to refer to later. If the child has an SSEN, then during an annual review you will be asked about the child's progress, significant steps forward and difficulties they have faced. Keeping a weekly record of things you and an LSA have observed is an excellent resource for you, other professionals, parents, carers and the child's next teacher or school. This sort of record need not take much time. Brief notes which can be referred to easily under headings would be the best, for example:

| Name | Week beginning |
|---|---|
| Literacy | |
| Numeracy | |
| Other curriculum areas | |
| Personal and social | |

Anyone who is involved in the child's learning should be able to contribute to this record, and it would be useful for the parents to see and comment upon it on a regular basis.

Within the language unit where I worked each child had a home/school book which went to and fro between home and school. Whenever there was anything that needed to be mentioned that had happened at home, or concerns noted at school, it would be jotted down in the book. In this way we could keep track of any problems and it was a useful record to refer back to at a later date. Another use for the book was to forward messages that the children had been asked to pass on when we were unsure whether they would remember to tell someone or be able to relate it accurately.

Setting up regular meetings with the parents (fortnightly or monthly depending on the need) can assist both of you in knowing what progress is being made, in which areas and whether there is any change in the child as a result. Keeping these meetings regular can help you to determine your next steps and you will be able to plan for the child more effectively. The importance of parental involvement wherever possible cannot be over-emphasised. If you work alongside one another, sharing your common concerns and triumphs together, then the child will be at a great advantage.

As with any child with specific educational needs, you will need to allow the parents access to the IEPs you write and, if possible, enable them to contribute towards this planning. If meeting up is difficult, then a brief telephone call will also help. However you discuss the child, keep notes on any occasion about what you discussed and the steps you have proposed to take next. It will jog your memory and will be useful evidence for the future.

## SPEECH AND LANGUAGE THERAPISTS

The other important professionals in the lives of these children are SLTs. Without them you will struggle to provide adequately for the child in your care. Within a mainstream setting, the amount of time you spend with these therapists is extremely limited and very precious. The more information you can share with them and the more you ask, the better the relationship will be. More often than not, they will see the child in school and will then leave work for you to continue until their next visit. Try to ensure that you have time to discuss this programme with the therapist and if possible take your LSA along too, because it is most likely that she will do the bulk of the one-to-one work with the child. If you do not ask for help or raise specific issues when they are in school, then your opportunity for support will be lost.

SLTs are very specific about the work they do or don't do in school, and it is important to understand the role they play in a school setting. The main things SLTs do not do and will not give advice on is elocution, the altering of dialects, literacy problems, public speaking skills or minor articulation difficulties (such as a child confusing 'th' and 'f').

They will see children where there is concern over their speech, language or communication skills and they will assess their development in these areas. They will generally be able to give you a diagnosis of the problem and plan the intervention needed to enable the child to develop certain skills. They can provide advice and training for parents and teachers working with the child. Once this is established, then they will evaluate the progress the child is making and will set IEPs of their own, outlining the work to be carried out. Their aim is to work closely with parents, carers and the other professionals working with the child, but time can be limited and you may be unable to contact them easily once they are out of school.

SLTs work as part of a multi-disciplinary and multi-agency team and they sometimes have their own specific language assistants (SLAs) who may be able to come to work in school with your children. If they have SLAs, they will manage them and provide the work they have to teach the children. They will write reports after their initial assessment, for SEN procedures and for annual reviews. As well as providing written reports for annual reviews, therapists will always be invited to attend the annual review. They will also take part in case conferences and some may even be able to join you for parents' evenings.

If necessary, they will refer a child to another agency if it is not appropriate to give them speech and language therapy. They will also be able to give you advice about alternative or augmentative communications skills you can teach the children they support. Their skills, like teachers', are constantly being updated as they attend study days, and any new information can be shared between you.

SLTs have a wealth of experience which you can draw upon, and their professional advice is essential so that you may develop the child's skills to their maximum potential. From my experience, I could not have managed without SLTs, and the support I received from them was reflected in my teaching and planning for the children I taught. As teachers, we do not have all the knowledge necessary to understand the underlying language and communication problems of a child or the correct and appropriate way to remediate them.

## EDUCATIONAL PSYCHOLOGISTS

Educational psychologists are often in and out of schools on a fairly regular basis and are an invaluable resource. They may be able to offer practical suggestions and support for the children in your class. Their knowledge of psychological theories and research enables them to be able to teach you techniques to help children who may have learning difficulties or emotional problems.

Most educational psychologists are employed by local education authorities, and these are the ones you are most likely to encounter. They will provide reports and advice for you to follow and are usually able to attend annual reviews. Some are self-employed and you may find parents who have paid for an independent assessment before waiting for a school referral. This may be the case where the statementing procedure has taken a long time or the parents have had to fight harder for their child to be formally assessed when they were very young. Use all the knowledge you have from any evidence to help you build a picture of the child's development over time.

These professionals work mainly with parents, teachers, social workers, doctors and education officers. It would be helpful to enable the parents and educational psychologists to meet before or after a child's assessment, in order that they can mutually benefit from sharing their worries and concerns and discuss the next steps that need to be taken. Do not forget that, as well as having specific language problems, these children will have social and emotional needs that need to be addressed, and this is where an educational psychologist can potentially help most.

## OCCUPATIONAL THERAPISTS

OTs work with people who have physical, mental and/or social problems. Some of these people have difficulties as a result of their birth, and other problems are caused by accidents or an illness. OTs' primary aim is to enable their patients to live as independently as possible. They help people to achieve their full potential at work, school and in their leisure time.

Not all children with language impairment need to be seen by an OT, but some do need additional support. The most common problems OTs deal with are developing motor control skills, both fine and gross. They will set a programme of activities with the child and these can be carried out by an LSA on a one-to-one basis. The children often need help with daily living skills such as dressing. Some children may have sensory integration difficulties and problems with visual perception, and an OT is able to help with these problems.

## ALL SUPPORT

This will give you an idea of the support you may receive with the language-impaired children in your class, and may even spark off some ideas of your own. Use and adapt all ideas to suit your own teaching style and the organisation of your own classroom. The most important thing to remember is to share your expertise with the other staff in the school, and never be afraid to ask for advice. There is so much more support, advice and help available for higher profile specific educational needs, and language impairment is a much more common problem than it may appear. There is a relative lack of advice or training for children with these problems, and therefore all teaching staff should be more aware of them and be more prepared to manage them.

Language-impairment need not be considered as a severe handicap to a child's learning ability. Just because children have comprehension or articulation difficulties, it does not mean that their intellectual ability is impaired. These children may be frustrated and hampered by their difficulty, but your challenge is to help them to unlock their full potential and achieve to the best of their ability, whatever stage they have reached in their academic life.

# GLOSSARY

APHASIA – inability to express thought in words

ASPERGER'S SYNDROME – a form of autism

DYSARTHRIA – a motor speech disorder that leaves someone unable to articulate speech

DYSFLUENCY – the loss of ability to control the smooth flow of speech production, resulting in, for example, hesitancy, poor rhythm or stuttering

DYSLEXIA – a language disorder which affects the ability to read

DYSGRAPHIA – a language disorder that primarily affects the ability to write

ECHOLALIA – the automatic repetition of all or part of what someone has said

LANDAU KLEFFNER SYNDROME – a neurological disorder which affects the parts of the brain controlling comprehension and speech

LANGUAGE DISORDER – a serious abnormality in the system underlying the use of language

LINGUISTICS – the science of language

MORPHEMES – the smallest meaningful unit in the grammar of a language

MORPHOLOGY – the study of word structure, especially in terms of morphemes

PARAPHASIAS – the production of unintended syllables, words, or phrases during the effort to speak

PHONETICS – the science of speech sounds, especially of their production, transmission and reception

PHONOLOGY – the study of the sound systems of languages

PRAGMATICS – the study of the factors influencing a person's choice of language

SEMANTICS – the study of linguistic meaning

SPEECH DISORDER – a serious abnormality in the system underlying the use of spoken language

SPEECH IMPAIRMENT – a regular, involuntary deviation from the norms of speech

SYNTAX – the study of word combinations; the study of sentence structure

WORD-FINDING PROBLEM – inability to retrieve a desired word, symptomatic of aphasia

# REFERENCES

Adams, C. (1990) *Syntactic comprehension in children with expressive language impairment.* British Journal of Disorders of Communication 25, 149–71.

Bishop, D. and Rosenbloom, L. (1987) *Classification of Childhood Language Disorders.* In Yule, W. and Rutter, M. (Eds.) *Language Development and Disorders.* Oxford: MacKeith Press/Blackwell.

Donaldson, M.L. (1995). *Children with Language Impairments. An Introduction.* London and Bristol, Pennsylvania: Jessica Kingsley Publishers.

Lloyd, S. (1992) *The Phonics Handbook: A Handbook for Teaching Reading, Writing and Spelling.* Chigwell: Jolly Learning.

Rapin, I. and Allen, D. (1983) *Developmental Language Disorders: nosological considerations.* In Kirk, U. (ed.) *Neuropsychology of Language, Reading and Spelling.* New York: Academic Press.

Rapin, I. and Allen, D.A. (1987) *Developmental dysphasia and autism in preschool children: characteristics and subtypes.* In *Proceedings of the First International Symposium on Specific Speech and Language Disorders in Children,* University of Reading: AFASIC.

Rinaldi, W. (1998) *Language Concepts to Access Learning.* Chilworth: Wendy Rinaldi.

(1999) National Numeracy Strategy. DfEE.

(1998) *National Literacy Strategy.* DfEE.

(2005) *Reviewing the Frameworks for teaching Literacy and Mathematics.* DfES.

# FURTHER READING

Baddeley, A. (1990) *Human Memory, Theory and Practice.* Hove & London (U.K.), Hillsdale (U.S.A): Lawrence Erlbaum Associates.

Berk, L. (1997) *Child Development* (Fourth Edition). Boston: Allyn and Bacon.

Bryant, P. and Bradley, L. (1985) *Children's Reading Problems.* Oxford: Blackwell.

Bull, S. and Solity, J. (1987) *Classroom Management: Principles to Practice.* London: Croom Helm.

Crystal, D. (1997) *The Cambridge Encyclopaedia of Language.* Cambridge: Cambridge University Press.

Desforges, C. (ed) (1996) *An Introduction to Teaching: Psychological Perspectives.* Oxford: Blackwell.

Dockrell, J. and McShane, J. (1991) *Children's Learning Difficulties: A Cognitive Approach.* Oxford (U.K.) Cambridge (U.S.A.): Blackwell.

Eysenck, M.W. and Keane, M.T. (1995) *Cognitive Psychology: A Student's Handbook.* Hove: Lawrence Erlbaum Associates.

Gathercole, S.E. and Baddeley, A.D. (1993) *Working Memory and Language.* Hove: Lawrence Erlbaum Associates.

Hampshire County Council. (1998) *Principles of the TEACCH model.*

Holt, J. (1983) *How Children Learn.* London: Penguin Books.

Howe, M. (1984) *A Teacher's Guide to the Psychology of Learning.* Oxford: Blackwell.

Hulme, C. and Mackenzie, S. (1992) *Working Memory and Severe Learning Difficulties.* Hove: Lawrence Erlbaum Associates.

Kail, R. (1990) *The Development of Memory in Children* (Third Edition). New York: Freeman.

Law, J. Ed., (1994) *Before School. A Handbook of Approaches to Intervention with Preschool Language-impaired Children.* London: AFASIC.

Lees, J. and Urwin, S. (1998) *Children With Language Disorders.* (Second Edition). London: Whurr Publishers Ltd.

Martin, D. and Miller, C. (1996) *Speech and Language Difficulties in the Classroom.* London: David Fulton Publishers.

Mogford-Bevan, K. and Sadler, J. (eds) (1995) *Child Language Disability, Implications in and Educational Setting.* Newcastle-Upon-Tyne: Egghead Publications.

Reason, R. and Boote, R. (1997) *Helping Children With Reading and Spelling. A Special Needs Manual.* London and New York: Routledge.

Snowling, M. (ed) (1994) *Children's Written Language Difficulties – Assessment and Management*. London: Routledge.

Tizard, B. and Hughes, M. (1984) *Young Children Learning: Talking and Thinking At Home and At School*. London: Fontana

Wood, D. (1988) *How Children Think and Learn*. Oxford: Blackwell.

Yule, W. and Rutter, M. (eds), (1993) *Language Development and Disorders*. London: MacKeith Press.

# USEFUL WEBSITES

All these websites were correct at the time we went to press.

## ADHD Owner's Manual

*http://www.edutechsbs.com/adhd*

This website is a privately owned site with clear information about ADHD and how teachers can tackle it within the classroom.

## Afasic

*http://www.afasic.org.uk*

Afasic is a parent-led organisation which helps children and young people with speech and language impairments, and their families. They provide information and training for parents and professionals.

## Association of Educational Psychologists

*http://www.aep.org.uk*

In the careers section of this website you will find an overview of the role of an Educational Psychologist and the type of problems they encounter with the children they work with.

## Badger Publishing

*http://www.badger-publishing.co.uk*

You can find information on the books and reading resources available in book boxes from this publisher.

## British Association of Occupational Therapists

*http://www.baot.co.uk*

This website gives information about occupational therapy and an overview of how it can help different groups of people.

## Centre for Literacy in Primary Education

*http://www.clpe.co.uk*

The CLPE is a charitable trust which provides an educational centre for schools, teachers, parents, teaching assistants and other educators.

## I-Can

*http://www.ican.org.uk*

I-Can is a charity which helps children with speech and language difficulties across the UK.

## Jolly Phonics

*http://www.jollylearning.co.uk*

This gives an overview of the Jolly Phonics programme and the accompanying resources to use for teaching. There is also information about the Jolly Grammar programme and Jolly Readers.

## Makaton Vocabulary Development Project

*http://www.makaton.org*

This website gives you information about Makaton signing and where you can find a course to learn it. It also provides a contact for getting advice for families.

## National Curriculum Online

*http://www.nc.uk.neet*

The attainment targets and programmes of study for each subject and key stage can be found on this site.

## Oxford Reading Tree

*http://www.oup.co.uk/oxed/primary/ort*

You can find information about this reading scheme and its resources. There is a section of advice and resources for teachers and an online section for children.

## Royal College of Speech and Language Therapists

*http://www.rcslt.org*

There is an area on this website which enables you to find out about the role of the speech and language therapist and the type of patients they work with.

## The Standards Site, Primary National Strategy

*http://www.standards.dfes.gov.uk/primary*

This website is the main site of the Department for Education and Skills and enables you to find resources and curriculum information. It has links to literacy and numeracy curriculum details and programmes of study.